Together for Life

Together for Life

A Preparation for Marriage and for the Ceremony
by Joseph M. Champlin

Scripture Readings
Comments for Couples
Texts for the New Marriage Rite

Ave Maria Press Notre Dame Indiana

First printing, March, 1970
Twenty-seventh printing, March, 1983
2,700,000 copies in print

Revised edition, 1979

Nihil Obstat: John L. Reedy, C.S.C.
              Censor Deputatus

Imprimatur: Most Rev. Leo A. Pursley, D.D.
              Bishop of Fort Wayne-South Bend

Design: Mike Rider

Photos: Cover, Pages 30-31, 89, Rohn Engh
        Pages 2-3, Bro. Martinus, C.S.C.
        Pages 70-71, Justin Soleta
        Page 54, Kenneth Bethel
        Pages 50-51, John David Arms
        Pages 8-9, 79, H. Armstrong Roberts

Printed in the United States of America

Contents

Introduction

The commentaries in *Together for Life* were written by people who, like you, are in love. True enough, the hand, the words, the style belong to a priest. But the ideas and inspiration came from many married persons, engaged couples and other individuals who over the past 23 years have opened their hearts to me and sketched a picture of what marriage both is and should be. To all of them, and to one person in particular who shared in the work and writing of this book I am very grateful.

It was created not only by, but also for persons in love. Very soon you intend to tell the whole world of your mutual feelings. Before God and before others you will promise to love until death, to live together for life. That will be *your* day, *your* wedding.

Since the nuptial ceremony centers around the two of you, it is only natural for you both to participate actively in the service and to plan the details. The new marriage ritual for Catholics makes that possible and we hope this book makes it easier for you as it has for some two million couples who have used the text before you.

All of the authorized readings, prayers, prefaces and blessings are here, as well as some comments which should prove of interest to a man and a woman about to marry. It is for you to study the material, then select the texts you like best and mark those choices on the companion selection form. They have been arranged according to the order of the ceremony. You may employ other scriptural passages not in this booklet if you wish.

The priest or deacon who will officiate at your wedding certainly should be pleased with this interest. Moreover, he can help in preparing for that happy occasion when you will be joined as one and will agree to honor and cherish each other all the days of your life.

Entrance Rite

Opening Prayer

A-1*

Father,   106**
you have made the bond of marriage
a holy mystery,
a symbol of Christ's love for his Church.
Hear our prayers for N. and N.
With faith in you and in each other
they pledge their love today.
May their lives always bear witness
to the reality of that love.

We ask you this
through our Lord Jesus Christ, your Son,
who lives and reigns with you and the Holy Spirit,
one God, for ever and ever.

A-2

Father,   107
hear our prayers for N. and N.,
who today are united in marriage before your altar.
Give them your blessing,
and strengthen their love for each other.

We ask you this
through our Lord . . .

A-3

Almighty God,   108
hear our prayers for N. and N.,
who have come here today
to be united in the sacrament of marriage.
Increase their faith in you and in each other,
and through them bless your Church
    (with Christian children).

We ask you this
through our Lord . . .

A-4

Father,   109
when you created mankind
you willed that man and wife should be one.
Bind N. and N.
in the loving union of marriage;
and make their love fruitful
so that they may be living witnesses
to your divine love in the world.

We ask you this
through our Lord . . .

---

*The Marriage Rite Card number
**Number in Ritual

7

A-1* The Creation of Man and Woman (774-1)**

Genesis 1:26-28, 31a

God said, "Let us make man in our own
image, in the likeness of ourselves, and
let them be masters of the fish of the sea,
the birds of heaven, the cattle, all the
wild beasts and all the reptiles that crawl
upon the earth."

*God created man in the image of himself,
in the image of God he created him,
male and female he created them.*

God blessed them, saying to them, "Be
fruitful, multiply, fill the earth and
conquer it. Be masters of the fish, the
birds of heaven and all living animals on
the earth."

God saw all he had made, and indeed it
was very good.

This is the word of the Lord.

---

*The Marriage Rite Card number
**The Lectionary number for this reading

"Indeed it was very good"

Strange how some persons in every age have tried to make the body bad and sex evil. The two of you certainly do not feel that way. Your love is very special, a beautiful experience, probably the most wonderful event so far in your life. Deep down you must be thinking that anything so beautiful, so wonderful, simply has to come from God. And you are right.

It is not really God's fault that we continue to take a negative view of our bodies and our sexual lives. People have been reading this biblical passage for thousands of years. The words and message are clear enough. We came forth from God's creative hand; he made our minds, our hearts, our bodies; we resemble the Lord, we are like him, we were fashioned in his own image. God's comment on his own creation of man should remove all doubts from our mind: "Indeed it was very good."

But God gave us from the beginning a certain additional blessing, a partial sharing in his power to create and rule the world. A partial sharing, that is, because the Lord rather effortlessly made us and governs the universe. It takes effort, however, for men and women to do these things.

For example, when you cooperate with God to create new life, a new person, you will do so by making joyous, ecstatic love together. But that lovemaking is an energetic, even exhausting act. Then both of you will suffer through the difficulties and pains of pregnancy and childbirth. Yet the labor will not be over when your baby utters its first cry. To care for this child, to train your young children, to teach them how to love as you now love takes years. It requires patience, hard work and, above all, self-sacrificing love.

Husband and wife, however, do not face this future alone. God who created, who shares his powers with men and women, promises to stand by them. Struggle the couple must, but with a serenity built on confidence that the Lord who is love and who does all things easily will be with them always and in every effort.

B-2 **The Creation of Woman** (774-2)

Genesis 2:18-24

The Lord God said, "It is not good that the man should be alone. I will make him a helpmate."

So from the soil the Lord God fashioned all the wild beasts and all the birds of heaven. These he brought to the man to see what he would call them; each one was to bear the name the man would give it.

The man gave names to all the cattle, all the birds of heaven and all the wild beasts. But no helpmate suitable for man was found for him.

So the Lord God made the man fall into deep sleep. And while he slept, he took one of his ribs and enclosed it in flesh.

The Lord God built the rib he had taken from the man into a woman, and brought her to the man.

The man exclaimed:

"This at last is bone from my bones,
and flesh from my flesh!
This is to be called woman,
for this was taken from man."

This is why a man leaves his father and mother and joins himself to his wife, and they become one body.

This is the word of the Lord.

Different But Equal Helpmates

Most of us don't enjoy going to the movies alone or eating by ourselves or being isolated in a large city. Many also would prefer to live with another person or with other people rather than to set up separate housekeeping. Are we simply reflecting here God's word, "It is not good that the man should be alone"?

In any case, from the very beginning the Lord has made it possible for us to share our lives with another, to have a "helpmate" if we so choose. That partner is flesh of our flesh, bone of our bone, a person, equally human, equally precious in the sight of God and others.

The Lord's wise ways, however, made this helpmate not only an infinitely mysterious individual, but also a fascinatingly different kind of person. We joke about this, even write songs about it. "How to handle a woman" or "Why can't a woman be more like a man?" Still the fact remains that a man never fully understands a woman, nor does a woman ever totally comprehend the thoughts, feelings and actions of a man.

Yet together we form a marvelous blend. Like two halves of a whole we complement one another, fulfill each other's needs, make up mutual deficiencies. In a word, we are equal but different.

Our grasp of those real differences between the sexes probably grows most rapidly in courtship and marriage. Day after day being together, living together, gradually reveals the real individual. We play fewer games as the relationship develops. It is to be hoped we also come to recognize that the man is first a unique person and only then a male, that the woman is likewise a distinct individual first and only later a female.

Do you seem to be aggressive and competitive, need to feel superior, grow discouraged easily, deal with generalities, ignore details, reason logically and objectively, keep feelings inside? Many would say these are the general traits of a man in our contemporary culture. Do you seem to manifest a capacity for endurance, be disposed to love, hate more easily, be concerned with details, think intuitively, show feelings with ease, be more religious? Many would claim these are the typical characteristics of a woman in today's society.

Others, however, maintain those are false stereotypes, artificial images putting pressure on every man and woman to conform, to act in this so-called masculine way or that so-called feminine manner. Critics of such categorizations would like to break down what they judge as merely contrived standards for men and women, thus allowing every person the freedom to be his or her individualized self.

Lovers like you should be able to resolve this question without difficulty. For love means, among other things, seeing and cherishing one's partner as a unique person, deep, rich, different. It is to view each other as equal, but complementing helpmates.

The Meeting of Isaac and Rebekah (774-3)

Genesis 24:48-51; 58-67

The servant of Abraham said to Laban:
"I blessed the Lord, God of my master
Abraham, who had so graciously led me
to choose the daughter of my master's
brother for his son.

Now tell me whether you are prepared to
show kindness and goodness to my
master; if not, say so, and I shall know
what to do."

Laban and Bethuel replied, "This is from
the Lord; it is not in our power to say yes
or no to you.

Rebekah is there before you. Take her
and go; and let her become the wife of
your master's son, as the Lord has
decreed."

They called Rebekah and asked her, "Do
you want to leave with this man?" "I do,"
she replied. Accordingly they let their
sister Rebekah go, with her nurse, and
Abraham's servant and his men.

They blessed Rebekah in these words:

*"Sister of ours, increase
to thousands and tens of thousands!
May your descendants gain possession
of the gates of their enemies!"*

Rebekah and her servants stood up,
mounted the camels, and followed the
man. The servant took Rebekah and
departed.

Isaac, who lived in the Negeb, had
meanwhile come into the wilderness of
the well of Lahai Roi.

Now Isaac went walking in the fields as
evening fell, and looking up saw camels
approaching.

And Rebekah looked up and saw Isaac.
She jumped down from her camel, and
asked the servant, "Who is that man
walking through the fields to meet us?"
The servant replied, "That is my master";
then she took her veil and hid her face.

The servant told Isaac the whole story,
and Isaac led Rebekah into his tent and
made her his wife; and he loved her. And
so Isaac was consoled for the loss of his
mother.

This is the word of the Lord.

A Time of Independence

When the bride walks down the aisle, meets the groom and the two stand before an altar it is not uncommon for parents to shed a few tears. These are happy-sad tears. Happy because this is a joyous occasion, a moment in which their son or daughter, while nervous and uncertain, still exudes contentment and happiness. But these are sad tears too, for a certain melancholy sorrow also hangs heavy over parental hearts.

A child's marriage forms for some as it were the final cutting of the umbilical cord, a total release from the family womb. The parents' task is over. Now they can only sit back, watch, and hope that their years of loving concern and careful training have produced a mature young man or woman, one capable of adjusting to the demands of married life.

The wedding may contain a note of finality for the son or daughter as well. It signifies the time of dependence upon parents has ended (although this independence may have started sometime earlier) and the period of interdependence upon a partner has begun. This beginning of a new existence together with one we love means facing life as it is, sharing joys with one another, and sorrows as well. There should be no turning back now, no clinging to childhood or adolescent crutches.

This is easier said than done. Linus holds on for dear life to his security blanket. He fears standing alone, on his own two feet. We laugh at him and approve of Lucy's impatience with his immature thumb-sucking and blanket-clutching. But deep down we feel a rather constant tug to do the same, an inclination to return to the protective shelter of the home, a tendency to run and seek the comfort of father or mother when things get rough.

To do so in marriage, however, means marital misery and sows the seed for possible future disaster.

Isaac took Rebekah as his wife, loved her, and was consoled in the loss of his mother. Certainly spouses should be consolation to each other in time of trial and source of support for each other in periods of anxiety. Nor does mature independence as a married couple exclude tender love and care for both sets of parents. But a husband is not meant to replace one's father; a wife is not to substitute for one's mother.

The husband who constantly compares wife to mother invites a harsh rebuke. "I am not your mother, I am your wife." The wife who frequently makes similar comparative allusions to her father can expect the same response. "I am not your father, I am your husband."

Love for parent, love for partner. Both loves are good, both are needed, but they are different and must not be confused.

The Marriage of Tobias and Sarah (774-4)

Tobit 7:9c-10, 11c-17

Then Tobias said to Raphael, "Brother Azarias, will you ask Raguel to give me my sister Sarah?"

Raguel overheard the words, and said to the young man, "Eat and drink, and make the most of your evening; no one else has the right to take my daughter Sarah —no one but you, my brother. In any case, I, for my own part, am not at liberty to give her to anyone else, since you are her next of kin. However, my boy, I must be frank with you."

Tobias spoke out, "I will not hear of eating and drinking till you have come to a decision about me." Raguel answered, "Very well. Since, as prescribed by the Book of Moses, she is given to you, heaven itself decrees she shall be yours. I therefore entrust your sister to you. From now you are her brother and she is your sister. She is given to you from today for ever. The Lord of heaven favour you tonight, my child, and grant you his grace and peace."

Raguel called for his daughter Sarah, took her by the hand and gave her to Tobias with these words, "I entrust her to you; the law and the ruling recorded in the Book of Moses assign her to you as your wife. Take her; take her home to your father's house with a good conscience. The God of heaven grant you a good journey in peace."

Then he turned to her mother and asked her to fetch him writing paper. He drew up the marriage contract, how he gave his daughter as bride to Tobias according to the ordinance in the Law of Moses.

After this they began to eat and drink.

This is the word of the Lord.

Today and Forever

In a short while you will stand before priest, relatives, friends, face one another, hold each other's hands, and promise to share your lives together "until death do us part." This is a permanent commitment to love and honor one another in good times and in bad, in poverty and in plenty, in sickness and in health, for better or for worse. These are serious words and solemn vows.

Too serious and too solemn, perhaps, for some in our modern world. A growing number of persons—including some prominent figures of our society who are thus very much in the public eye—ask, "Why marry? Why not simply live together? Why commit yourself to anything more binding than a mutual agreement, a promise to maintain a living-together relationship only so long as it remains acceptable to both partners involved?" And it is hardly a secret that many are doing just that, living together without any concern for a marriage contract or for binding nuptials.

This attitude or opinion carries with it a certain logic and wisdom. After all, should couples no longer compatible wage a daily cold or hot war and end up destroying each other?

But it has a major weakness also.

A great part of the joy of an engagement and a marriage is the sense of security which goes with it, a feeling of being loved and wanted and needed, a realization that someone cares for us—on a permanent basis.

One young lady remarked that her goal in life is to love and understand, to be loved and understood. She hopes that this ideal will be realized in all persons with whom she comes in contact, but she seeks it especially in that intimate relationship with the man who will be by her side until death.

A newspaperman and film critic, married over 25 years, yet quite understanding of those in the motion picture business whose marital or domestic careers have often been less successful than their professional ones, still feels that only in the stress and strain of a permanent commitment does the real character of each person develop. The love and responsibilities demanded by such an enduring promise supply an opportunity for the full depth of a relationship between husband and wife to materialize.

All of this is dull, impractical, unrealistic talk for the two of you in love. *Your* marriage will never fail, *your* love never waver, your commitment *never* be questioned. In these blissful, but sometimes blind days of courtship, you naturally think only in terms of forever and ever.

However, the rising divorce rate, the talk about temporary commitments, the unwillingness to persevere when difficulties arise should make you pause and ponder. A marriage that lasts for life demands love and loyalty, God's grace and peace.

B-5 **Prayer of the New Spouses** (774-5)

Tobit 8:4-9

**Tobias rose from the bed, and said to
Sarah, "Get up, my sister; You and I
must pray and petition our Lord to win
his grace and his protection." She stood
up, and they began praying for protection,
and this was how he began:**

*"You are blessed, O God of our fathers;
blessed, too, is your name
for ever and ever.
Let the heavens bless you
and all things you have made
for evermore.*

*It was you who created Adam,
you who created Eve his wife
to be his help and support;
and from these two the human race was
born. It was you who said,
'It is not good that the man should be
alone; let us make him a
helpmate like himself.'
And so I do not take my sister
for any lustful motive;
I do it in singleness of heart.
Be kind enough to have pity on her and
on me and bring us to old age together."*

This is the word of the Lord.

Praying Together

I wonder how many newlyweds begin their first evening on the honeymoon praying together as Tobias and Sarah did. It certainly establishes a good pattern for the future. However, unless the couple began some form of common prayer during courtship days, the possibilities of praying together on their wedding night would be quite slim.

Perhaps we should ask you as a man and a woman preparing for marriage a few very basic questions. Have you ever talked about God, about religion, about what you believe? Have you discussed your goals in life, what you hope to achieve, the values you hold most important? Have you spoken about children, about how you will raise them and what type of religious training they will receive? Hours of conversation about serious topics like these pave the way for prayer together.

Most Americans feel self-conscious about praying out loud with others in a personal way. We might rattle through the Lord's Prayer or recite a formal grace before meals, but to speak in our own words to God in the presence of a crowd or even with the one we love makes us ill at ease. We prefer private, silent moments for this sort of thing. Yet the times are changing.

Instructors in religion courses for Catholic students spend time now training young persons how to pray spontaneously and vocally. God is our father and Jesus our brother, the pupils are told, and we should speak to them easily, naturally, informally. In time, these students will be in your position and prayer together as a couple should be much easier for them.

Still the path to common prayer for the two of you should not be unusually difficult. Worshiping together on Sunday probably is the best start. If you both are Catholic, then participating in Mass and receiving the Eucharist can become a weekly meeting with God and with each other at the altar. Grace or blessing at meals might be another occasion for learning how to pray as a couple. The standard, memorized formula surely is acceptable; however, making up a personal blessing, taking turns composing it, extending the prayer to encompass other gifts and concerns beyond the table could lead easily to similar prayer outside of mealtime. To end an evening with a simple, short prayer to "win God's grace and his protection" may seem like the dreamy preaching of a priest, but I doubt it.

Marriage means a great sharing of selves. To pray together opens up a new and deeper level of this sharing. We now consciously bring the Lord into our love and our love into the sight of God. To pray is to place your life, your lives in our Father's hands. It is to listen to him, to be open to his Word, to make yourselves available to his will, to respond willingly to his desires for you as an individual and for you as a couple.

B-6 Love Is Strong as Death (774-6)

Song of Songs 2:8-10, 14, 16a; 8:6-7a

THE BRIDE

I hear my Beloved.
See how he comes
leaping on the mountains,
bounding over the hills.
My Beloved is like a gazelle,
like a young stag.

See where he stands
behind our wall.
He looks in at the window,
he peers through the lattice.

My Beloved lifts up his voice,
he says to me,
"Come then, my love,
my lovely one, come.

My dove, hiding in the clefts of the rock,
in the coverts of the cliff,
show me your face,
let me hear your voice;
for your voice is sweet
and your face is beautiful."

My beloved is mine and I am his.
He said to me:

Set me like a seal on your heart,
like a seal on your arm.
For love is strong as Death,
jealousy relentless as Sheol.
The flash of it is a flash of fire,
a flame of the Lord himself.

Love no flood can quench,
no torrents drown.

This is the word of the Lord.

Staying in Love

A young woman very much involved with a man, but wondering if she was following the right course, recently wrote: "Pray that I won't turn off the light when it comes. Love is so painful and absorbing that one can prefer blindness."

Falling in love means a beautiful face, a sweet voice, a handsome body, a charming personality. It means running up the steps to meet your girl and standing in the window as he drives away at the end of a date. It means lazy dreams of a future with him and a restless urge to be at home with her. Falling in love is indeed lovely, lovely, lovely. But is it real?

Time tells. As the months pass this blind, compulsive, divorced-from-reality experience of falling in love either grows into something strong and deep or withers, then dies. When young lovers come down from the clouds, their vision improves. They notice faults, disagree on decisions, argue or fight. They stop playing games, act more naturally, let their hair down. The true you comes out.

Sometimes these are moments in the death of love. The breakup for a few is bitter, quick and hurtful; for others, it is a gradual drifting apart, a slow realization that what seemed so eternal, sure and clear was only first love, or infatuation, or the longing of a lonely person. Love in these cases just dies.

But not always. Often love grows, building on that strong initial attraction and developing deeper daily. It blossoms, it gains strength, it becomes strong as death.

Faults remain, but come to be accepted; disagreements continue, but are resolved through compromise; arguments go on, but end with reconciliation. The road gets rocky at times and for periods the couple may even drift off in different directions. But eventually they return, resume the journey and find their mutual love has plunged to a new and richer level.

The man and woman who have weathered falling in love, have gone through the slow and uneven route of growing in love are now ready to stay in love. He still climbs those stairs, more often, more regularly, although less rapidly. He stays later, too, hating to say good-bye, happy simply to be in her presence, content to share his life and thoughts with this marvelous person. She still watches in the window, still feels sad to see him go. But now reassured that he will return in a few hours, knowing that soon he will seal their love with a promise, that soon she will say, "My beloved is mine, and I am his."

B-7 **A Really Good Wife** (774-7)

Sirach 26:1-4, 16-21

Happy the husband of a really good wife;
the number of his days will be doubled.

A perfect wife is the joy of her husband,
he will live out the years of his life in
peace.

A good wife is the best of portions,
reserved for those who fear the Lord;

rich or poor, they will be glad of heart,
cheerful of face, whatever the season.

The grace of a wife will charm her
husband,
her accomplishments will make him the
stronger.

A silent wife is a gift from the Lord,
no price can be put on a well-trained
character.

A modest wife is a boon twice over,
a chaste character cannot be weighted
on scales.

Like the sun rising over the mountains of
the Lord
is the beauty of a good wife in a well-kept
house.

This is the word of the Lord.

A Happy Husband

In a sound marriage both husband and wife must put away their blankets, face reality, and develop a mature independence. It is a wife you marry, not a mother; a husband, not a father. Yet every marital relationship entails a certain dependence, a mutual leaning on one another. There are times when the wife in fact does play the role of mother and the husband, in turn, occasionally does act as a father.

Three familiar, ancient words, "I love you," warm a person's heart. However, three others, "I need you," can totally conquer it.

A woman, for example, earnestly desires to be loved and needed. Yet she may feel drawn to a strong man, admires a man with self-confidence, finds most attractive a take-charge type of guy. The suitor who seems too dependent upon her, too desperately in love with her, too helpless without her somehow loses appeal.

True enough, women often marry persons simply because these men need them and wives even persevere in rather difficult situations merely because they are needed by unloving husbands. Generally, however, a woman prefers a man who wants to live with her, needs to live with her, but who perhaps could live without her. We cannot deny the challenge element involved in most marriages.

A man reacts in much the same way. He, too, seeks to be loved and needed. He may visualize himself as the family protector, the source of support, the one cool under pressure. But this husband also has deep emotional requirements. He enjoys having his wife comfort him, likes it when she rubs his back, looks for her ego-bolstering encouragement when work and the world get him down. Nevertheless, if she clings too tightly, If she makes him her only concern and their family her only interest, he becomes uneasy.

All of this means that matrimony, like all of life, is a mystery. Successful marriages demand a mysterious blending of mature independence and loving dependence. A happy husband learns when he must be courageous and self-reliant, when he needs humbly, gratefully to accept the warm support of his wife. A really good wife comes also to know when she must stand alone and unaided, when she needs the steady, supportive arm of her husband.

Learning and knowing how to combine these two apparently contradictory tendencies take most of one's life. And we never really master the process. But couples who have worked at it, who mix the two with good results, live out their years in peace. Rich or poor, they are glad of heart, cheerful of face, whatever the season.

B-8 The New Covenant of the People of God (774-8)

Jeremiah 31:31-32a, 33-34a

See, the days are coming—it is Yahweh who speaks—when I will make a new covenant with the House of Israel (and the House of Judah), but not a covenant like the one I made with their ancestors on the day I took them by the hand to bring them out of the land of Egypt.

No, this is the covenant I will make with the House of Israel when those days arrive—it is the Lord who speaks. Deep within them I will plant my Law, writing it on their hearts. Then I will be their God and they shall be my people.

There will be no further need for neighbour to try to teach neighbour, or brother to say to brother, "Learn to know the Lord!" No, they will all know me, the least no less than the greatest.

This is the word of the Lord.

A Sign of Our Marriage Vows

A ring on the third finger, left hand says something to people. It announces to all in stark terms that "He is married" or "She already has a husband." But for the giver and wearer, the wedding band means much more, carries far deeper implications. It is a sign of their nuptial vows, a visible reminder of their promise to love, to be faithful.

Most couples in the United States today seem to prefer the double-ring ceremony. And it does possess real advantages. Marriage is a giving-receiving relationship. The use of a ring for the bride and one for the groom perhaps more clearly symbolizes that notion. Both give, both receive a circular sign of this commitment to love and to honor until death.

An added personal gesture by the man and woman during this exchange of wedding bands can further stress that concept of giving-receiving. By placing the ring only part way on her finger as he pronounces the formula, he indicates his giving of himself to her. As she draws it on the rest of the way, his bride manifests her acceptance of that gift, of that commitment. Naturally this slight, but significant addition can be employed in either the single or double-ring service.

The gold or silver wedding ring, then, signifies some truths; it speaks to all, and to the couple especially, about love and matrimony. However, their very lives, their existence as husband and wife together is also a sign. The giving-receiving which should characterize every marriage symbolizes how God has and does deal with people, with men and women, with us.

In this reading we hear about the sacred contract, the new covenant which the Lord, Yahweh, made with his chosen people. "I will be their God and they shall be my people." He will guide them, protect them, comfort them. In return he expects their loyalty, their faith, their trust. He gives, they accept; he loves, they respond.

The same type of loving interchange should find its parallel in marriage. A husband buys his wife a corsage for Easter, takes her to dinner on their anniversary, finds a second job, signs up for special courses, understands when she, too, is tired at the end of her day or is off for another meeting at the school.

These are acts of love, deeds which demand an effort. He doesn't expect an equivalent return for every single gesture of giving. Marriage and love do not operate in such terms of justice or measured out responses. But she does and will reciprocate with faith, loyalty and trust. And this is really what he wants.

The wife gives also. She cooks his favorite dish, remains patient when the unexpected makes him late for dinner, endures a sometimes frustrating all-day confinement to house and children, juggles the conflicting demands of her husband, her children, her home, her job.

These acts are equally loving, equally taxing. She does not anticipate an exact return on this investment of giving either. But her hope is to have, keep, deepen his loyalty and faith and trust.

The giving-receiving relationship between God and his people can be an example, even an inspiration for married people. But just as the wedding ring is a sign of their vows, so their mutual love, their own giving-receiving, tells the world of God's concern for us and how we should respond to that love.

Responsorial Psalm

C-1*   The Goodness of the Lord

PSALM 33:12 and 18, 20-21, 22 (776-1)**

Leader: **The earth is full of the goodness of the Lord.**

All: The earth is full of the goodness of the Lord.

**Happy the nation whose God is Yahweh,
the people he has chosen for his heritage.
But see how the eye of Yahweh is on those who fear him,
on those who rely on his love.**

All: The earth is full of the goodness of the Lord.

**Our soul awaits Yahweh,
he is our help and shield;
our hearts rejoice in him,
we trust in his holy name.**

All: The earth is full of the goodness of the Lord.

**Yahweh, let your love rest on us
as our hope has rested in you.**

All: The earth is full of the goodness of the Lord.

---

*The Marriage Rite Card number
**The Lectionary number for this reading

C-2   Bless the Lord

PSALM 34:2-3, 4-5, 6-7, 8-9 (776-2)

Leader: **I will bless the Lord at all times.**
Or: **Taste and see the goodness of the Lord.**

All: I will bless the Lord at all times.
Or: *Taste and see the goodness of the Lord.*

**My soul glories in Yahweh,
let the humble hear and rejoice.
Proclaim with me the greatness of Yahweh,
together let us extol his name.**

All: I will bless the Lord at all times.
Or: *Taste and see the goodness of the Lord.*

**I seek Yahweh, and he answers me
and frees me from all my fears.
Every face turned to him grows brighter
and is never ashamed.**

All: I will bless the Lord at all times.
Or: *Taste and see the goodness of the Lord.*

**A cry goes up from the poor man, and Yahweh hears,
and helps him in all his troubles.
The angel of Yahweh pitches camp round those who fear him; and he keeps them safe.**

All: I will bless the Lord at all times.
Or: *Taste and see the goodness of the Lord.*

**How good Yahweh is—only taste and see!
Happy the man who takes shelter in him.
Fear Yahweh, you his holy ones:
those who fear him want for nothing.**

All: I will bless the Lord at all times.
Or: *Taste and see the goodness of the Lord.*

C-3 The Lord Is Kind

PSALM 103:1-2, 8 and 13, 17-18a (776-3)

Leader: **The Lord is kind and merciful.**
Or: *The Lord's kindness is everlasting to those who fear him.*

All: The Lord is kind and merciful.
Or: *The Lord's kindness is everlasting to those who fear him.*

Bless Yahweh, my soul,
bless his holy name, all that is in me!
Bless Yahweh, my soul,
and remember all his kindnesses.

All: The Lord is kind and merciful.
Or: *The Lord's kindness is everlasting to those who fear him.*

Yahweh is tender and compassionate,
slow to anger, most loving.
As tenderly as a father treats his children,
so Yahweh treats those who fear him.

All: The Lord is kind and merciful.
Or: *The Lord's kindness is everlasting to those who fear him.*

Yet Yahweh's love for those who fear him
lasts from all eternity and for ever,
like his goodness to their children's children.
as long as they keep his covenant.

All: The Lord is kind and merciful.
Or: *The Lord's kindness is everlasting to those who fear him.*

C-4 Happy the Man

PSALM 112:12, 3-4, 5-7a, 7bc-8, 9 (776-4)

Leader: **Happy are those who do what the Lord commands.**
Or: **Alleluia.**

All: Happy are those who do what the Lord commands.
Or: *Alleluia.*

Happy the man who fears Yahweh
by joyfully keeping his commandments!
Children of such a man will be powers on earth,
descendants of the upright will always be blessed.

All: Happy are those who do what the Lord commands.
Or: *Alleluia.*

There will be riches and wealth for his family
and his righteousness can never change.
For the upright he shines like a lamp in the dark,
he is merciful, tenderhearted, virtuous.

All: Happy are those who do what the Lord commands.
Or: *Alleluia.*

Interest is not charged by this good man,
he is honest in all his dealings.
Kept safe by virtue, he is ever steadfast,
and leaves an imperishable memory behind him;
with constant heart, and confidence in Yahweh.

All: Happy are those who do what the Lord commands.
Or: *Alleluia.*

He need never fear bad news.
Steadfast in heart he overcomes his fears:
in the end he will triumph over his enemies.

All: Happy are those who do what the Lord commands.
Or: *Alleluia.*

Quick to be generous, he gives to the poor,
his righteousness can never change,
men such as this will always be honored.

All: Happy are those who do what the Lord commands.
Or: *Alleluia.*

C-5 Happy All Those

PSALM 128:1-2, 3, 4-5 (776-5)

Leader: **Happy are those who fear the Lord.**
Or: **See how the Lord blesses those who fear him.**

All: *Happy are those who fear the Lord.*
Or: *See how the Lord blesses those who fear him.*

**Happy, all those who fear Yahweh
and follow in his paths.
You will eat what your hands have worked for,**
happiness and prosperity will be yours.

All: *Happy are those who fear the Lord.*
Or: *See how the Lord blesses those who fear him.*

**Your wife: a fruitful vine
on the inner walls of your house.
Your sons: round your table
like shoots round an olive tree.**

All: *Happy are those who fear the Lord.*
Or: *See how the Lord blesses those who fear .him.*

**Such are the blessings that fall
on the man who fears Yahweh.
May Yahweh bless you from Zion
all the days of your life!**

All: *Happy are those who fear the Lord.*
Or: *See how the Lord blesses those who fear him.*

C-6 The Lord Is Compassionate

PSALM 145:8-9, 10 and 15, 17-18 (776-6)

Leader: **The Lord is compassionate to all his creatures.**

All: *The Lord is compassionate to all his creatures.*

**He, Yahweh, is merciful, tenderhearted,
slow to anger, very loving,**
**and universally kind; Yahweh's tenderness
embraces all his creatures.**

All: *The Lord is compassionate to all his creatures.*

**Yahweh, all your creatures thank you,
and your faithful bless you.
Patiently all creatures look to you
to feed them throughout the year.**

All: *The Lord is compassionate to all his creatures.*

**Righteous in all that he does,
Yahweh acts only out of love,**
**standing close to all who invoke him,
close to all who invoke Yahweh
faithfully.**

All: *The Lord is compassionate to all his creatures.*

C-7 Praise the Lord

PSALM 148:1-2, 3-4, 9-10, 11-12ab,
    12c-14a (776-7)

Leader: **Let all praise the name of the Lord.**
Or: *Alleluia.*

All: Let all praise the name of the Lord.
Or: *Alleluia.*

Let heaven praise Yahweh:
    praise him, heavenly heights,
praise him, all his angels,
    praise him, all his armies!

All: Let all praise the name of the Lord.
Or: *Alleluia.*

Praise him, sun and moon,
    praise him, shining stars,
praise him, highest heavens,
    and waters above the heavens!

All: Let all praise the name of the Lord.
Or: *Alleluia.*

Mountains and hills,
    orchards and forests,
wild animals and farm animals,
    snakes and birds.

All: Let all praise the name of the Lord.
Or: *Alleluia.*

All kings on earth and nations,
    princes, all rulers in the world,
young men and girls,
    old people, and children too!

All: Let all praise the name of the Lord.
Or: *Alleluia.*

Let them all praise the name of Yahweh,
    for his name and no other is sublime,
transcending earth and heaven in majesty,
    raising the fortunes of his people.

All: Let all praise the name of the Lord.
Or: *Alleluia.*

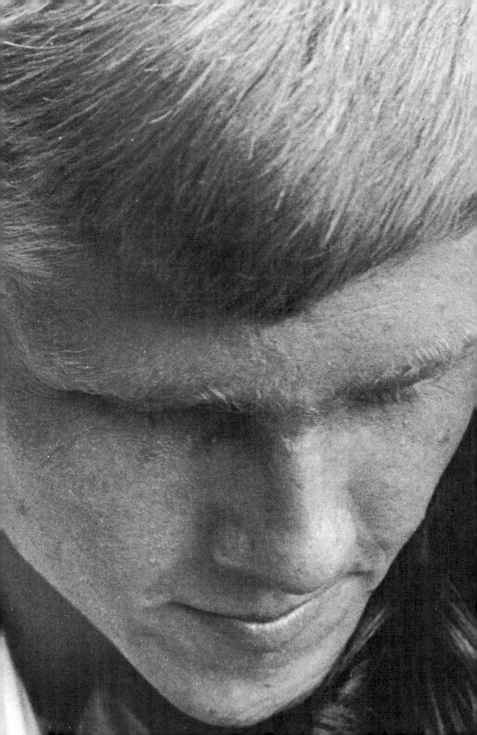

D-1* **The Love of Christ** (775-1)**

Romans 8:31b-35, 37-39

With God on our side who can be
against us?

Since God did not spare his own Son,
but gave him up to benefit us all, we may
be certain, after such a gift, that he will
not refuse anything he can give. Could
anyone accuse those that God has
chosen?

When God acquits, could anyone
condemn? Could Christ Jesus? No! He
not only died for us—he rose from the
dead, and there at God's right hand he
stands and pleads for us.

Nothing therefore can come between us
and the love of Christ, even if we are
troubled or worried, or being persecuted,
or lacking food or clothes, or being
threatened or even attacked.

These are the trials through which we
triumph, by the power of him who loved
us.

For I am certain of this: neither death
nor life, no angel, no prince, nothing that
exists, nothing still to come, not any
power, or height or depth, nor any
created thing, can ever come between us
and the love of God made visible in
Christ Jesus our Lord.

This is the word of the Lord.

---

*The Marriage Rite Card number
**The Lectionary number for this reading

Who Can Ever Come Between Us?

One Sunday a priest walked outside and around the parish church during Mass and came upon a couple by the main entrance. The young man was standing with a two-year-old son in his arms. The young woman was sitting on the steps, head bent over and face in her hands. The heat and crowd combined with morning sickness had made her feel faint and dizzy. The patience of this husband and the distress of his wife mirror more accurately the real world of marriage than a dreamy, trouble-free portrait sketched by romanticists.

Weddings are and should be occasions filled with joy and laughter. But we also need to prepare the bride and groom for *both* the mountains *and* the valleys of married life. A paragraph from the exhortation in the old ritual summarizes rather well that total picture.

"This union then is most serious, because it will bind you together for life in a relationship so close and so intimate that it will profoundly influence your whole future. That future, with its hopes and disappointments, its successes and its failures, its pleasures and its pains, its joys and its sorrows, is hidden from your eyes. You know that these elements are mingled in every life and are to be expected in your own. And so, not knowing what is before you, you take each other for better or for worse, for richer or for poorer, in sickness and in health, until death."

No one knows exactly what form those disappointments, failures, pains, sorrows will take, nor how bitter, nor how permanent. Will it be the discovery of a baby born with physical defects or the slow realization that your child is blind or deaf or mentally retarded? Will it be the mistake of a teenage son or daughter with the accompanying broken heart and keen disappointment? Will it be a wife's arthritic lameness in her leg or a husband's disconsolate feelings about his work?

We can conjecture about when and what kind and why. But not about their coming. This is certain.

Yet these burdens can never steal away our peace. They cannot tear us away from God. As long as our love for Christ remains constant, we will not experience abandonment or unhappiness. Pain, yes, but unhappiness, no. Jesus' death on the cross not only assures us of his constant love, it also supplies us with reason for hope. The Lord conquered suffering and death; we, through faith and love, will also as a couple share his victory over pain and death.

Nor can these difficulties tear us away from one another. Real love, as we have seen, is strong as death. The husband and wife who truly love each other need fear neither death nor life, neither anything that exists nor anything still to come. Their death-defeating, cross-conquering mutual love will merely grow through afflictions.

A crucifix in the home serves as a constant reminder of these truths. It tells of Jesus' suffering, his victory, his love for us. It speaks of the share every couple must have in the Lord's death and resurrection. It reminds us that with love for Christ and for one another nothing can come between us, even if we are troubled or worried, or being persecuted, or lacking food or clothes, or being threatened or even attacked. These are the trials through which we triumph, by the power of him who loved us.

D-2 **The Life of a Christian** (775-2)

Short version: Romans 12:1-2, 9-13
Long version: Romans 12:1-2, 9-18

verses 1-2

Think of God's mercy, my brothers, and
worship him, I beg you, in a way that is
worthy of thinking beings, by offering
your living bodies as a holy sacrifice,
truly pleasing to God.

Do not model yourselves on the
behaviour of the world around you, but
let your behaviour change, modelled by
your new mind. This is the only way to
discover the will of God and know what
is good, what it is that God wants, what
is the perfect thing to do.

verses 9-13

Do not let your love be a pretense, but
sincerely prefer good to evil.

Love each other as much as brothers
should, and have a profound respect for
each other.

Work for the Lord with untiring effort and
with earnestness of spirit.

If you have hope, this will make you
cheerful. Do not give up if trials come;
and keep on praying.

If any of the saints are in need you must
share with them; and you should make
hospitality your special care.

verses 14-18

Bless those who persecute you; never
curse them, bless them.

Rejoice with those who rejoice and be
sad with those in sorrow.

Treat everyone with equal kindness;
never be condescending but make real
friends with the poor. Do not allow
yourself to become self-satisfied.

Never repay evil with evil but let
everyone see that you are interested only
in the highest ideals.

Do all you can to live at peace with
everyone.

This is the word of the Lord.

Sharing Our Love With Others

It is dangerous for a young girl to think she will "reform" a boyfriend with seriously bad habits and it is equally risky for a man to believe he can correct deeply undesirable traits in a woman he dates. Still, we often change for the better after falling in love. Lovers do influence one another and many times bring out the best in each other.

This begins early in our adolescent years. The teenager infatuated with an initial love may for the first time in his young life think about someone else. He buys her presents, carries her books home, spends hours talking with her on the telephone. He is learning about love, about how happiness can come from getting out of yourself and becoming concerned about another. Young girls, of course, undergo the same experience.

The two of you left that tender, important, but premature love behind long ago. Yours is a quiet, more secure, a lasting type of love which has as its goal the happiness of the other. However, it may be time for you both to consider the extension of this mutual love beyond yourselves. Your prime desire naturally is to make each other happy; but this may be impossible unless you open your hearts to the world around you, unless you become concerned about making others happy.

Benedictine monks have a motto: "When a guest comes, there Christ comes." You haven't set up housekeeping yet, but you soon will. To display Christian hospitality, to welcome a guest, however inconvenient or unexpected, represents a basic start on the road to a mutual outgoing love for others.

"Rejoice with those who rejoice and be sad with those in sorrow." This advice from St. Paul advances that love another step. To be at funerals or visit the hospital, to attend weddings or serve as a godparent—these may cut into free time and cause personal hardship. But if we take the Lord's words seriously about doing these things to the least of our brothers, we can hardly neglect them.

Later, in marriage, you both will face the need constantly to reevaluate decisions about time and energy for community activities. A family that is too self-centered ultimately will fail to grow as it should; a family that is overextended in outside efforts, on the other hand, will find love at home deteriorating. So volunteer work with the community and the Church is needed and valuable; so are extra hours at the office and on the road. But we easily slip into extremes at either end. The question then must frequently be posed, "My time, am I spending too much or too little at home, at the office, at the church, at the community organization?"

In these days, concern for the poor, for those less fortunate must also enter into the marriage picture. To push ourselves alone, to manipulate others, to seek only our own family's welfare is hardly the Christian ideal. Legitimate ambition and justifiable pride for and in the family have their place, but they must not be achieved at the expense of others.

We need have no fears. To love others outside the family, to give in the right way will not harm the love between husband and wife. When you began to love your partner, you gave, but in the giving you gained more. So, as a couple, your love and giving to those outside the home will enable your own love as husband and wife to grow stronger and deeper.
God keeps his word.

D-3 Your Members Are Temples of the Holy Spirit (775-3)

I Corinthians 6-13c-15a, 17-20

The body—this is not meant for fornication; it is for the Lord, and the Lord for the body.

God, who raised the Lord from the dead, will by his power raise us up too.

You know, surely, that your bodies are members making up the body of Christ.

But anyone who is joined to the Lord is one spirit with him.

Keep away from fornication. All the other sins are committed outside the body; but to fornicate is to sin against your own body.

Your body, you know, is the temple of the Holy Spirit, who is in you since you received him from God.

You are not your own property; you have been bought and paid for. That is why you should use your body for the glory of God.

This is the word of the Lord.

Why Wait?

Serious, but temporary, challenges deserve our concern, but should be kept in proper perspective. The question of why wait until marriage before making complete love together fits into that category for you, a couple soon to exchange nuptial vows. It is a serious but temporary difficulty.

As love grows between two people so does the desire to express those tender, inner feelings in a physical way. They wish to hold, touch, possess, to yield, to surrender, to relieve frustration, to give peace and satisfaction. What complicates the matter is the beauty of sexual intercourse and of the love-play which prepares for it. Persons who have tasted this joy—and current statistics suggest that in a group preparing for marriage many already have anticipated some marital lovemaking—wonder why so beautiful an act should be wrong. It seems to deepen their love, bring them closer together, make them very happy.

Still, good reasons do exist for waiting, or for bringing feelings under control in case you haven't waited.

The risk of self-deception and the danger of selfishness always lurk near us. When a man and a woman have enjoyed sexual intercourse or deep intimacies on a regular basis, what they think is the kind of love needed to sustain a lifelong relationship may be only the physical, emotional closeness and elation which accompanies complete or nearly complete lovemaking. Strong and good as these feelings are, they tend to diminish in time and will not carry a couple over the hurdles of married life.

Most persons entertain at least a few doubts about the strength of their present love and the outcome of their future marriage. Frequent indulgence in pre-marital intercourse can intensify those uncertainties. This anticipation may lead the man or woman to wonder if it is a body one craves, not a person. In nervously hesitant moments alone, the future spouses may wonder if they are loved as individuals or only because they have totally given themselves to the other in a physical way.

Then, too, the struggle to wait essentially means an effort to develop self-discipline and self-control. These qualities certainly will be needed after the nuptial vows (before and after pregnancy, during illness, when work or war separates the couple). When they are present in the courtship there is a good possibility they will remain in the marriage.

The major point, however, centers on the matrimonial promises. A marriage is not a marriage until two people before God and others, the Church and the State, solemnly pledge love and fidelity to each other. Before that instant minds can change, rings be returned, plans cancelled. But once the solemn contract has been made, husband and wife embark on a venture which demands that they love and be faithful to one person alone. Sexual intercourse reserved for the marriage bed tends to solidify that vow and place it in the context of a mutual promise. It then becomes something special.

To sum up: If you have waited this long, then hang on a bit longer and don't let anyone or anything talk you out of it. If you haven't, don't be anxious. Sex before the wedding doesn't guarantee a happy marriage, nor does it necessarily mean an unhappy one. The past isn't terribly important right now; what counts is the present and how you dispose yourself for the future.

The Greatest of These Is Love (775-4)

I Corinthians 12:31-1-13:8a

Be ambitious for the higher gifts. And I
am going to show you a way that is
better than any of them.

If I have all the eloquence of men or of
angels, but speak without love, I am
simply a gong booming or a cymbal
clashing.

If I have the gift of prophecy, understanding all the mysteries there are, and
knowing everything and if I have faith in
all its fulness, to move mountains, but
without love, then I am nothing at all.

If I give away all that I possess, piece by
piece, and if I even let them take my
body to burn it, but am without love, it
will do me no good whatever.

Love is always patient and kind; it is
never jealous; love is never boastful or
conceited; it is never rude or selfish; it
does not take offense, and is not resentful.

Love takes no pleasure in other people's
sins but delights in the truth; it is always
ready to excuse, to trust, to hope, and to
endure whatever comes.

Love does not come to an end.

This is the word of the Lord.

Communication

Many marriage counselors believe that communication heads the list of essential ingredients for a successful marriage. Conversely, they maintain that lack of or poor communication tops the causes of marital discord and disaster.

What is this communication? Like all profound realities of life, it defies a clear and exact definition. For marriage we might describe communication as a sympathetic sharing of inner feelings with each other. It means letting her know when you are down or angry; pleased and content; letting him realize you have been hurt or feel neglected, are happy and secure.

Verbal communication may be the obvious form, but it is not necessarily the most effective method of communicating. Yet we do and must use words. I tell her what I think or I get this gnawing tension off my chest. I bring something out into the open or tell him what has been bothering me.

Still words often impede rather than facilitate communication. Sometimes there is even an experience of utter frustration when we try to verbalize inner sentiments of love and tenderness only to discover that these cannot be adequately expressed in words. Then, too, confusion enters in and misunderstanding as well. Words may fail to convey my feelings or my partner interprets what was said in a way I never intended. When we are hesitant or afraid to speak honestly and when we are hostile or irritated, our words become charged with double meanings, sarcasm, anger. So words alone don't always succeed.

Lovers, however, communicate in many ways. Through touch, for example. Satisfying sexual intercourse naturally can express in complex fashion love and caring, repentance and forgiveness. Yet quite simple gestures may be equally filled with feeling for a couple. A husband touches his wife's arm at a happy moment or kisses her on the forehead. She fingers the hair at the base of his head or rests her hand on his knee as they drive along. These touches talk.

So do our eyes. The doorways to a person's soul, someone once said. They can betray delight or sorrow, a happy spirit or hurt feelings. A sensitive man or woman detects how the partner truly feels even if there is an attempt to bluff one's way through situations with casual words or an effort to conceal emotions with a pretense of stoicism. Couples not only speak to each other with their eyes, they also unwittingly disclose with their glances the relationship developing between them. Observant friends swiftly note a loving look or admiring gaze.

As mutual love matures, a man and a woman find it less necessary to speak, to touch, to look, to strive consciously at every moment for communication. It often is quietly there. In those situations, each one knows, senses how the other feels. Each one comes intuitively to read the other's mood. And both discover a form of deep communicating by mere presence. Just being together, in silence, provides occasions for a sharing of inner feelings that is as deep as it is mysterious.

D-5 The Mystery of Marriage (775-5)

Short version: Ephesians 5:2a, 25-32
Long version: Ephesians 5:2a, 21-33

verse 2a

Follow Christ by loving as he loved you.

verses 21-24

Give way to one another in obedience to Christ. Wives should regard their husbands as they regard the Lord,

since as Christ is head of the Church and saves the whole body, so is a husband the head of his wife;

and as the Church submits to Christ, so should wives to their husbands, in everything.

verses 25-32

Husbands should love their wives just as Christ loved the Church and sacrificed himself for her to make her holy.

He made her clean by washing her in water with a form of words, so that when he took her to himself she would be glorious, with no speck or wrinkle or anything like that, but holy and faultless.

In the same way, husbands must love their wives as they love their own bodies; for a man to love his wife is for him to love himself.

A man never hates his own body, but he feeds it and looks after it; and that is the way Christ treats the Church,

because it is his body—and we are its living parts.

For this reason, a man must leave his father and mother and be joined to his wife, and the two will become one body.

This mystery has many implications; but I am saying it applies to Christ and the Church.

verse 33

To sum up; you too, each one of you, must love his wife as he loves himself; and let every wife respect her husband.

This is the word of the Lord.

A Sign of God's Grace

In the recently revised form of Mass, the priest pours wine and a little water into the cup, then says: "By the mystery of this water and wine, may we come to share in his divinity who humbled himself to share in our humanity."

Drops of water disappear into the wine. The two mix. They symbolize a mysterious blending of the divine and human in Jesus Christ. God the Father so loved us that he gave his Son, sent him into the world for us. Christ, even though he was God, consented to become man for our sake. In a sense this was a marriage between God and us, between the spiritual and the material, between this world and the next.

Just as the Father's love has been demonstrated by his sending of the Son into the world, so Jesus' concern for us was made clear once and for all by the total giving of himself on the cross. There can be no greater love than for a person to lay down his life on behalf of another. This is the epitome of unselfishness, the perfect example of self-giving love.

Marriage stands as a sign of the covenant between Yahweh and the chosen people of the Old Testament. The present reading from St. Paul also makes it perfectly clear that the love between a man and a woman also resembles the love which God the Father and Jesus Christ have for us. The married couple should find in the Father's love and the Savior's giving encouragement to love without reserve in their own lives. At the same time, from the joy they discover in loving each other the same two can come to understand better what it means to say that the Father loves us or that Jesus died to save all.

Yet the mystery of marriage goes even beyond this. For believing Christians matrimony is a sacrament, a visible sign of God's invisible grace and of his presence in our lives. The sign itself of this particular sacrament is not a formula of words combined with water, wine, bread or oil. Instead, it is the mutual promise between bride and groom and the life lived in accordance with that nuptial vow.

Practical consequences flow from the sacramental nature of marriage. If the sign of the sacrament is this promise and the living out of the promise, then it follows that every time you are faithful, tender, considerate, every time you compromise or reconcile, every time you are thoughtful or unselfish, God's grace enters your lives. Each time Christ becomes present in your midst, each time the Holy Spirit dwells in your hearts and in your home.

People enjoy visiting married couples who truly love each other. They radiate happiness, peace, contentment. Those visitors sense a certain divine presence in the house, they feel God is there in that home.

D-6 Live in Love and Thanksgiving (775-6)

Colossians 3:12-17

You are God's chosen race, his saints; he
loves you, and you should be clothed in
sincere compassion, in kindness and
humility, gentleness and patience.

Bear with one another; forgive each other
as soon as a quarrel begins. The Lord
has forgiven you; now you must do the
same.

Over all these clothes, to keep them
together and complete them, put on love.

And may the peace of Christ reign in
your hearts, because it is for this that
you were called together as parts of one
body. Always be thankful.

Let the message of Christ, in all its
richness, find a home with you. Teach
each other, and advise each other, in all
wisdom. With gratitude in your hearts
sing psalms and hymns and inspired
songs to God;

and never say or do anything except in
the name of the Lord Jesus, giving
thanks to God the Father through him.

This is the word of the Lord.

Reconciliation

Love and trust walk hand in hand. As your feelings and love for each other grew, so did your trust. Isn't that true for you as a man about to marry? Didn't you begin to have confidence in this wonderful woman and wish to entrust her with your secrets and sorrows, your accomplishments and anxieties? Did you sense a great desire to tell her everything about yourself? Do you even now want her to know about your past?

And you, the bride-to-be. Aren't love for and trust in him almost interchangeable terms? Haven't you also wanted him to share all of your past? Have you worried about telling him certain things? Do you today want to, but wonder if it is wise?

Determining what of the past to confide and how to do it are hard, often agonizing decisions for any man or woman in love. Both wish to be truly honest and hold nothing back. Yet can he, can she accept these confessions? Some persons simply are not strong enough to do so. Is he, is she? Ultimately each individual must decide alone. He or she must weigh the past, the partner, the potential harm or benefit such trusting revelations hold for the future. Nevertheless, it should be evident that to blurt out all without consideration is at once naive and unwise.

The fact remains, however, that young lovers do trust and do open up their lives to one another. Herein lies the joy and the risk of love itself. Not to love is to surround oneself with a protective shell and to insulate the heart from harm. But it also consigns us to a closed existence, shuts us off from others, keeps us from fully tasting life. At the same time, to love, to trust, to reveal oneself renders us vulnerable and exposes soft spots in our emotional armor.

You love this woman and because of her trust you now know how to hit where it hurts the most. And you have responded to this man's love and accepted his intimate confidences. You, too, know how to wound him deeply. In the course of your life together you both will, only occasionally we hope, do just that—hurt each other.

Why? Who can answer that question? We bring pain instead of pleasure to a loved one for many reasons. Because we are tired or troubled by something else, feel pressure at work or misunderstand something done or left undone. Frequently, small, stupid points prick our patience; the wet towel left on the bathroom floor, the delay caused by a partner who is always late. In any event, we do throughout the course of an argument make hurtful remarks and touch sore areas. We injure that very person in this world we love the most.

But all is not lost. Mutual love can and should soar to a new level after one of these disagreements. If reconciliation follows quickly (never let the sun go down on your anger or climb into bed without making up), the healing goes beyond the hurt, the reconciling is more joyous than the suffering was painful. Afterwards, couples reach a deeper degree of acceptance, love and understanding.

Such reconciliation assumes a person is ready to forgive. Christ was and did. Couples need to follow his example.

Would this be a practical reminder fixed on the bathroom mirror or bedroom wall? "Bear with one another; forgive each other as soon as a quarrel begins. The Lord has forgiven you; now you must do the same."

D-7 **Peace and Harmony in the Family** (775-7)

I Peter 3:1-9

Wives should be obedient to their husbands. Then, if there are some husbands who have not yet obeyed the word, they may find themselves won over, without a word spoken, by the way their wives behave,

when they see how faithful and conscientious they are.

Do not dress up for show: doing up your hair, wearing gold bracelets and fine clothes;

all this should be inside, in a person's heart, imperishable: the ornament of a sweet and gentle disposition—this is what is precious in the sight of God.

That was how the holy women of the past dressed themselves attractively—they hoped in God and were tender and obedient to their husbands;

like Sarah, who was obedient to Abraham, and called him her lord. You are now her children, as long as you live good lives and do not give way to fear or worry.

In the same way, husbands must treat their wives with consideration in their life together, respecting a woman as one who, though she may be the weaker partner, is equally an heir to the life of grace. This will stop anything from coming in the way of your prayers.

Finally: you should all agree among yourselves and be sympathetic; love the brothers, have compassion and be self-effacing.

Never pay back one wrong with another or an angry word with another one; instead, pay back with a blessing. That is what you are called to do, so that you inherit a blessing yourself.

This is the word of the Lord.

Who Is Head of the House?

For many years before recent changes in the nuptial Mass, the bride and groom at a Catholic wedding heard as the first biblical reading only the words of St. Paul to the Ephesians. In his fifth chapter (see Reading D-5) he stresses that the husband is the head of the wife. Since he holds this position, she should regard him as she would the Lord. This means submission to him in everything and respect for him at all times.

True enough, Paul goes on to admonish the husband. He urges him to love his wife as he does his own body and to look after her, to care for her even at the cost of his life. But emphasis is on the wife's obedience and docility. Over the years, even centuries, this has been the normal role for a woman—to submit, to yield to men in general and to her husband in particular.

The feminine liberation movement seeks to correct that situation. Some of its leaders insist St. Paul disliked women and maintains his writings reflect this prejudice. Less bitter critics do not accuse him of this, but instead, they hold he was speaking to people of a particular generation and tailored his remarks to suit the customs of that time.

Yet both militant feminists and more moderate protagonists agree in their contention that we live today in a different world and in a new era. Women, they note, have won the right to vote and should be given equal opportunities in education and employment. Now, these people believe, women want equality in marriage.

Just how many women actually desire this kind of marital relationship is debatable. Most of the wives or brides-to-be I have known through over twenty years of work at the parish level and speak with even in these days tend to rely at least subconsciously and in the last analysis on the man for a final decision. They seem, deep down, to hope their husbands will take the lead and act as head of the house. At the same moment, they also want him to consider their own opinions and feelings before he comes to judgments of importance. Shared decision-making apparently is the desired goal.

The manner in which this works out during day-to-day married life apparently depends more upon the temperament of a couple and the matter under consideration than the theoretical question of who runs or who is head of the house.

In some, a husband clearly dominates; in most, the couple generally divide up minor decisions based on each person's special competence and talk through common, major concerns until some kind of consensus or satisfactory compromise is reached; in others, a wife may assume in practice the lead role although neither partner admits that fact in theory.

Throughout the getting to know you courtship period a couple should with great honesty seek to discover where they fit into this picture. That happens of course rather naturally, but sometimes a false understanding of love will keep one or both from manifesting displeasure felt at the way decisions are made.

Later, when the romantic glow fades and sober reality reigns, this unresolved problem of who decides and how can cause serious pain, even ultimate disaster.

St. Peter says: "Wives should be obedient to their husbands." He also adds, however, that "husbands must treat their wives with consideration in their life together, respecting a woman as one who, though she may be the weaker partner, is equally an heir to the life of grace."

How do you feel about those statements?

D-8 Love, Real and Active (775-8)

I John 3:18-24

My children,
our love is not to be just words or mere
talk,
but something real and active;

only by this can we be certain
that we are children of the truth
and be able to quieten our conscience in
his presence,

whatever accusations it may raise against
us,
because God is greater than our
conscience and he knows everything.

My dear people,
If we cannot be condemned by our
conscience,
we need not be afraid in God's presence,

and whatever we ask him,
we shall receive,
because we keep his commandments
and live the kind of life that he wants.

His commandments are these:
that we believe in the name of his Son
Jesus Christ
and that we love one another
as he told us to.

Whoever keeps his commandments
lives in God and God lives in him.
We know that he lives in us
by the Spirit that he has given us.

This is the word of the Lord.

D-9 God Is Love (775-9)

I John 4:7-12

My dear people,
let us love one another
since love comes from God
and everyone who loves is begotten by
God and knows God.

Anyone who fails to love can never have
known God,
because God is love.

God's love for us was revealed
when God sent into the world his only Son
so that we could have life through him;

this is the love I mean:
not our love for God,
but God's love for us when he sent his
Son
to be the sacrifice that takes our sins
away.

My dear people,
since God has loved us so much,
we too should love one another.

No one has ever seen God;
but as long as we love one another
God will live in us
and his love will be complete in us.

This is the word of the Lord.

A Failure to Communicate

Couples whose love has matured begin to communicate frequently in rather intuitive fashion. They sense the other's mood and often discover they are communicating by mere presence alone. However, good communication in marriage, indispensable for successful marital union, hardly ever just happens. It requires hard work, concentrated effort, patient struggling. But when two persons marry they commit themselves to that kind of life; they agree to a partnership in constant giving.

Some couples from the first days of courtship experience little difficulty with communicating. They are open, honestly reveal their true selves and easily convey sentiments of the heart. In fact, this leads them to conclude they love each other. However, as time moves on and they face the daily stress and strain of living together barriers may arise which weaken or destroy that spontaneous openness of earlier years. The following measures might help them and others restore or improve communication.

1. *Find the right time and place.* A young husband and wife who ran upon rocky ground after five years of marriage felt their root problem was this failure to talk together about anything, much less about the delicate and hard-to-discuss matters of inner feelings. In desperation they determined to spend at least 15 minutes each night after the children were in bed, talking with each other. The initial attempts were formal and awkward but gradually they moved from neutral areas to questions of vital, personal concern. This regular set-aside, quiet period succeeded for them.

2. *Be honest.* In our childhood days we learned to become defensive. We spoke out then in innocence and with candor only to have our hands slapped or feel parental displeasure. Thus we started to hide real, but unacceptable feelings within us and hoped in the process to avoid being hurt or punished. We concluded that speaking out costs too much. Now as adults in marriage we must reverse the process. A failure to communicate means precisely this—not honestly speaking out to a companion when we disagree, feel bad or neglected or whatever. It indeed does take courage to speak the truth. But as Jesus taught, the truth makes us free and leads to individual peace and marital harmony.

3. *Listen.* Dialogue involves an interchange of thoughts, words, feelings. We speak *and* listen. Communication by its nature presupposes a free flow *both* ways. Therefore, in either a planned communication session or one of those unrehearsed moments of real communicating, bring up your complaints with honesty, but be prepared to hear the other side. Seldom is one person totally at fault in anything. Few, if any, people are fundamentally ill-willed. Most interpersonal pain traces its origin to a misunderstanding, not to the intention of the one inflicting injury. If you try to understand *why* your partner said or did or failed to say or do something, the current sore spot and source of tension may appear in a totally different light.

4. *Let love prevail.* God commands all of us to love one another. We might say that this order from the Lord seems, from one point of view, superfluous for married persons. Death of their love means disaster in their marriage. Still our love and theirs must not be "just words or mere talk, but something real and active."

When such love dominates a marital relationship and pervades any period or moment of communication, our approach differs. The tone of voice is not high-pitched, loud or harsh. The heart is not closed, bitter or unforgiving. True, we entertain legitimate "gripes" and feel really "hurt." But we remain willing to understand and ready to change.

Love gives and forgives, accepts and adjusts. Persons who communicate well do the same.

D-10 **Marriage of the Lamb** (775-10)

Revelation 19:1, 5-9a

Happy are those who are invited to the wedding feast of the Lamb.

"I, John, seemed to hear the great sound of a huge crowd in heaven, singing, 'Alleluia! Victory and glory and power to our God!' "

Then a voice came from the throne; it said, "Praise our God, you servants of his and all who, great or small, revere him."

And I seemed to hear the voices of a huge crowd, like the sound of the ocean or the great roar of thunder, answering, "Alleluia! The reign of the Lord our God Almighty has begun; let us be glad and joyful and give praise to God, because this is the time for the marriage of the Lamb.

"His bride is ready, and she has been able to dress herself in dazzling white linen, because her linen is made of the good deeds of the saints."

The angel said, "Write this: Happy are those who are invited to the wedding feast of the Lamb."

This is the word of the Lord.

Alleluia Verse and Verse before the Gospel

E-1 *I John 4:8 and 11 (777-1)*

God is love; let us love one another as he has loved us.

E-2 *I John 4:12 (777-2)*

If we love one another God will live in us in perfect love.

E-3 *I John 4:16 (777-3)*

He who lives in love, lives in God, and God in him.

E-4 *I John 4:7b (777-4)*

Everyone who loves is born of God and knows him.

Dressed in Dazzling White

There are critics today who disdain the formality of American weddings. Some of these critics feel we should greatly simplify our marriage customs. They would eliminate the engraved invitations, omit bridal showers and stag parties, forget expensive wedding gowns and floral decorations, curtail the costly receptions.

They are, of course, correct in some respects. Nevertheless, the joining of two persons until death do them part *is* a significant moment. It should be celebrated, and surrounded with solemnity. This particular scriptural passage speaks of a mystical marriage in heaven, but the comments apply with equal force to every earthly wedding. "Let us be glad and joyful and give praise to God." "Happy are those who are invited to the wedding feast."

There are several ways and means which might give you and your guests a greater share in this moment of joy.

Participation leaflet. An inexpensively printed or mimeographed booklet could be handed to guests at the door and would contain the order of service, a citation of readings chosen (book, chapter, verses), the hymns and responses for all to sing or say, the names of the clergyman, organist, attendants, and perhaps also a personal message from the bride and groom.

Procession. A few couples recently have modified the customary wedding procession. Instead of the usual entrance by the bride on the arm of her father, the clergyman meets the bridal party at the door and then leads the bride, accompanied by her parents, and the groom, escorted by his father and mother, down the aisle to the sanctuary. Those favoring such an arrangement maintain it indicates in more effective fashion the gift of son or daughter to the prospective bride or groom.

Reader. The first readings from Scripture could be read by one or two persons close to the bride and groom (parents, relatives, attendants, friends).

Gifts. The new rite for Mass recommends procession in which the bread and wine and even suitable gifts for the poor are brought to the altar. The bride and groom could do this, or their parents, or predetermined members of the congregation.

Kiss of peace. After the Our Father the revised rules encourage some appropriate gesture signifying our love for and peace with one another. Once the celebrant invites the couple to exchange the kiss of peace, the bride and groom may then embrace and, when feasible, extend this greeting to the best man, maid of honor and others.

Comments. You might invite beforehand a representative from each family to prepare some brief remarks to be given as part of the homily or at the end of the service. In Quaker fashion, you could also welcome spontaneous comments from guests at a point near the ceremony's completion.

Communion from the cup. Early Christians normally received Communion, as we would say, "under both kinds." That is, they ate the Lord's body *and* drank his blood from the cup. For various complicated historical and doctrinal reasons this practice disappeared as a general custom many centuries ago. At the Second Vatican Council, the bishops decreed that on special occasions, and marriage is one of them, Catholics may once again drink the blood of Christ from the chalice.

How fitting for you, having just been joined together, to share the one blood of Christ from a common cup.

Liturgy of the Word
Gospel Readings and Comments

F-1* **The Beatitudes** (778-1)**

Matthew 5:1-12a

**Seeing the crowds, he went up the hill.
There he sat down and was joined by his
disciples.**

Then he began to speak. This is what he
taught them:

*"How happy are the poor in spirit:
theirs is the kingdom of heaven.*

*Happy the gentle:
they shall have the earth for their heritage.*

*Happy those who mourn:
they shall be comforted.*

*Happy those who hunger and
thirst for what is right:
they shall be satisfied.*

*Happy the merciful:
they shall have mercy shown them.*

*Happy the pure in heart:
they shall see God.*

*Happy the peacemakers:
they shall be called sons of God.*

*Happy those who are persecuted
in the cause of right:
theirs is the kingdom of heaven.*

*"Happy are you when people abuse you
and persecute you and speak all kinds of
calumny against you on my account.*

*Rejoice and be glad, for your reward will
be great in heaven."*

This is the gospel of the Lord.

---

*The Marriage Rite Card number
**The Lectionary number for this reading

Happiness Is

One warm and beautiful afternoon during his vacation a young married man, lazily bobbing in the salt water of the Atlantic Ocean, told how happy he was with his wife and family, how he sorely missed them when business trips took him away overnight.

A hard-working salesman, he had earned for his successful efforts in the previous year an expenses-paid week's midwinter vacation in Miami. His parent firm is a nationwide organization and nearly a hundred other winners joined him at this plush hotel with the very finest of entertainment and recreation facilities at their disposal. It was strictly a stag affair. That company (strangely, in my thinking) rewards the husband, but overlooks the wife. My companion confessed that after two days he was lonesome, unhappy, anxious to return home. And this in the face of luxurious accommodations and all the pleasures money could buy.

We seldom think of loneliness in connection with married people. We picture, instead, a soldier at an isolated outpost or a girl crying at home without a date for the dance. We imagine a spinster living alone in her orderly apartment or a bachelor eating by himself in a downtown restaurant.

But people in love, persons who have married may indeed feel the pang of loneliness more than any of these individuals. For they have experienced the joy of being together. They have shared much—a common bed and a common table, secret thoughts and special feelings, earnest hopes and fervent prayers. When separation comes, they sense a loss, a void. The greater their happiness as a couple, the more intense their suffering through separation.

A different, perhaps more painful loneliness occasionally creeps into married life. Regardless of how perfect the communication between husband and wife or how open and honest the daily dialogue, there will be times when some things cannot be shared. Those moments, thoughts, feelings are reserved for God alone. At an instance like this, you will recognize once again your companion as a unique, infinitely mysterious person, one never to be totally known or understood. That realization preserves the challenge element in marriage, but it also produces a certain frustration for those who wish to share all.

Likewise, gradual recognition that this life together on earth eventually must end can cloud our happiness. Some extremely moving episodes for me as a priest have taken place at hospitals and wakes, at funerals and cemeteries. To watch a couple grow old together, to be present when death steals away a partner of many years, to sense an empty heart during those days which follow is to view at once both the happiness and loneliness of real life.

Yet even then rays of hope shine through tears of grief. "Happy those who mourn: they shall be comforted." "Rejoice and be glad, for your reward will be great in heaven." The happiness felt on earth, glorious as it may be, represents only a sampling of the full, perfect, permanent joy later on. There, in my quite simple belief, we will somehow, sometime discover true and complete happiness— with God and with those we have loved on earth.

Salt of the Earth and Light of the World (778-2)

Matthew 5:13-16

Jesus said to his disciples:

**"You are the salt of the earth. But if salt
becomes tasteless, what can make it
salty again? It is good for nothing, and
can only be thrown out to be trampled
underfoot by men.**

**You are the light of the world. A city built
on a hilltop cannot be hidden.**

**No one lights a lamp to put it under a
tub; they put it on the lampstand where
it shines for everyone in the house.**

**In the same way your light must shine in
the sight of men, so that, seeing your
good works, they may give the praise to
your Father in heaven."**

This is the gospel of the Lord.

A Time to Remember

"What really scares the hell out of me is the fear I will someday start to take her for granted." These words of a first-year law student, married only two weeks earlier, reflect his concern for the future. He worries that later on he and she and they may become careless. His fear is well founded. The freshness of a new life together gradually does fade. Love can flourish in spite of this, but only if given constant cultivation.

Occasionally we need to stop and take stock. The time and place are not particularly important. A weekend retreat is fine, a Marriage Encounter perhaps even better. Or an evening for married persons. Or a quiet moment together looking back over the past months and years, asking real questions, giving frank answers. These might serve as starters.

Are we as much in love now as when we first married?

Am I?

If not, is it my fault?

Have I been faithful, have I trusted, have I believed?

Have we grown careless, taking each other for granted?

Am I too involved with my work?

Am I interested enough in his work? In her work?

Is our relationship with in-laws a thorny issue?

Do we communicate very well?

Do we easily share our inner feelings, both when we are happy and when we are hurt, when we are upset and when we are content?

Are family finances a sore spot?

Do disagreements become arguments, then battles, then wars?

Do we, at those times, often shout or swear or say vicious things?

Have we been willing to forgive? Have I?

Do we always make up before going to bed?

Has our sexual life been satisfying? If not, have we discussed it honestly and tried to improve?

Are we too self-centered as a family, not concerned enough about other families, about the Church, about the community in which we live?

Do we get away now and then, just the two of us?

Have we been good parents, loving, firm, understanding? Have I?

Has God slipped from our home?

Does the example we give lead our children to the Lord or take them away from their Maker?

Have we become selfish? Have I?

Am I, are we willing to begin again, to try harder, to give more?

F-3 House Built Upon a Rock (778-3)

Short version: Matthew 7:21, 24-25
Long version: Matthew 7:21, 24-29

Verse 21

Jesus said to his disciples:

**"It is not those who say to me, 'Lord,
Lord' who will enter the kingdom of
heaven, but the person who does the will
of my Father in heaven.**

Verses 24-25

**"Therefore, everyone who listens to these
words of mine and acts on them will be
like a sensible man who built his house
on rock.**

**Rain came down, floods rose, gales blew
and hurled themselves against that
house, and it did not fall: it was founded
on rock.**

Verses 26-29

**But everyone who listens to these words
of mine and does not act on them will be
like a stupid man who built his house
on sand.**

**Rain came down, floods rose, gales blew
and struck that house, and it fell; and
what a fall it had!"**

**Jesus had now finished what he wanted
to say, and his teaching made a deep
impression on the people**

**because he taught them with authority,
and not like their own scribes.**

This is the gospel of the Lord.

The Miracle of Life

People in love normally wish to share their happiness with the world. A woman who has just received her diamond feels like shouting. Bursting with joy and pride, she very likely will make it easy for people at work to notice that sparkling jewel on the third finger of her left hand. The man in love may react a bit less dramatically to this new feeling of love in his heart, but he, too, would like others to know what has happened. Love always reaches out beyond us.

It continues in marriage. Have you, like most engaged couples, dreamed happy dreams of a family and the moment when you will become parents? Most men possess a deep, powerful, yet often unconscious desire to be fathers. They want to prove their manhood, to beget a child, to leave offspring who will in a certain way preserve their own being after they leave this world. So also most women inwardly crave to conceive, carry, and bear a child. They want to bestow tenderness, warmth and care on that new person. They wish, in short, to be mothers.

Sexual intercourse is a highly intricate giving-receiving act. When conception results this marvelous interplay takes on a further dimension. Union of seed and ovum, coupled with God's mysterious cooperation and blessing, brings forth fresh human life into the world. The resulting child is not his, or hers, but theirs. Only the two of them could have created this unique individual, this wondrous being, unlike any other person in the entire universe. That son or daughter from the very beginning and forever will signify a special love which one man and one woman have for each other. The thought of all this and the responsibilities which accompany it can stagger the imagination. It should. For we are in fact speaking of a miracle.

Some afternoon the two of you might stop at a public library and dig up the July 22, 1966, issue of *Life*. An article with appropriate photographs describes the long months and unforgettable moments of pregnancy for a Swedish wife. "A Woman on Her Way to a Miracle" is its title and the author, Eleanor Graves, has beautifully captured the feelings of both mother and father as they experienced this miraculous event. The opening paragraph should whet your appetite.

Whatever feelings pregnancy may arouse —delight, indifference, resignation or horror—the very idea of creating a new human being is awesome. Pregnancy is surely the most creative thing you will ever do—even if you have done it inadvertently. And the process itself is miraculous—so hard to believe that at an already appointed hour you will divide like some ancient cell, and suddenly it won't just be you any longer but you and some other being, to whom you will be tied, by nerves and tissue and chemistry, all your life. This being is already within you, shouting in a sometimes deafening voice, look out, stand back, here comes a whole new person. And you are the lifeline, its substance, its nourishment. Only you can make sure that its bones are strong and its eyes are clear. How good you must be, how well behaved, how faithful to this being.

The sentiments of a father ought to be similar. When he studies the face of his newly born child, he cannot but think: This is flesh of my flesh, bone of my bone. Yet while the babe may one day look like me, think like me, even act like me, this tiny person will still become someone quite different from me. If I am good, if I am well behaved, if I try hard, perhaps the helpless infant will grow up to be strong and good and a little better person than I have been.

F-4 What God Has United, Man Must Not Divide (778-4)

Matthew 19:3-6

Some Pharisees approached him, and to test him they said, "Is it against the Law for a man to divorce his wife on any pretext whatever?"

He answered, "Have you not read that the Creator from the beginning made them male and female

and that he said: 'This is why a man must leave father and mother, and cling to his wife, and the two become one body?'

They are no longer two, therefore, but one body. So then, what God has united, man must not divide."

This is the gospel of the Lord.

How Far Should We Go?

This is another somewhat serious, but temporary challenge facing couples in love. Like the earlier question of "Why wait until marriage?" this decision about how far, short of sexual intercourse, a man and a woman should go in their premarital lovemaking will cease to be a significant issue after the wedding day. However, the matter does press upon many unmarried persons and causes them a bit of anxiety. We, therefore, should give it our attention, but avoid becoming obsessed with such a transitory problem.

Communication both in general and as it relates to a couple's sexual life needs to begin in the days before marriage. Yet one wonders if two lovers talk frankly about these intimate things. Have you, for example, as a couple, honestly discussed the whys and why nots of engaging in premarital sexual intercourse? And if you both came to a decision to postpone the bed until after the altar, have you openly talked about just how far your lovemaking before the wedding should go?

This type of communication eliminates guessing contests. The man no longer wonders how far will she let him go. The woman ceases to worry about how far does he want to go. Communicating like this eases much of the tension, clears the air, establishes mutually understood principles.

It also helps those who opt for waiting and for keeping emotions under fairly tight discipline. Our feelings vary tremendously, often inexplicably, from person to person and, within the same individual, from time to time. Quite often, on a given occasion, one of the partners seems in better control. In those instances, having clearly agreed on a path to be followed during courtship, the stronger of the two can remind the more aroused person of the previous agreement made at a less passionate moment.

All of the communicating in the world, however, doesn't eliminate the sometimes painful and frustrating struggle for emotional control during courtship. Nevertheless, engaged couples or couples dating seriously who sincerely seek to keep their feelings in reasonable check should not fret about specific sexual "rules" or even become anxious about isolated instances when matters got a little out of hand.

A very simple but apparently satisfactory guideline suggests that when one or both persons sense that the situation is getting a little overheated, becoming too involved, setting off the passions, it is time to come up for air. A few moments here to catch one's breath, say a few things, change positions can break the intense spell and quiet passionate desires.

Two people with a sense of humor will find the going much smoother. Passion is serious, single-minded, and will only rest when physical cravings are satisfied. Lovers who frequently laugh in the middle of a kiss or interrupt tender, affectionate embraces with a happy, humorous remark never give deep passion an opportunity to get started. For them waiting until that day when they will cling to each other and become one body is not easy, but their light and joyful sense of humor makes it less difficult.

F-5 Love, the Greatest Commandment (778-5)

Matthew 22:35-40

To disconcert him, one of them put
a question,

Master, which is the greatest
commandment of the Law?

Jesus said, "You must love the Lord your
God with all your heart, with all your
soul, and with all your mind.

This is the greatest and the first
commandment.

The second resembles it: You must love
your neighbor as yourself.

On these two commandments hang the
whole Law, and the Prophets also."

This is the gospel of the Lord.

Growth in Love

We entertain notions of what kind of person a friend or loved one should be; we also clearly know what type of individual we would like him to be. But when we truly love, we pass beyond both of these and accept the loved one simply as she or he is. We know the person well, the faults and virtues, the ups and downs, the positive points and the negative characteristics. I may not care for this or that aspect of your personality and I wish you would change here or improve there. Nevertheless, and more significantly, I take you as you stand before me, I love you just as you are.

That all sounds very poetic. Yet in day-to-day married life, such acceptance may not come easily. Acceptance demands effort and so does the adjustment which necessarily flows from it. You may note with surprise after a few weeks of living together that your wife has late-retiring, late-rising habits and even quickly accept this as an unchangeable part of her temperament. Later, how well will you adjust to the practical ramifications of that trait? Will you resent changing the diapers at 6:30 a.m., making your own breakfast and leaving for work without a farewell kiss? Maybe yes, maybe no. In either case the acceptance and adjustment required will cost you a bit.

Needless to say, these words apply equally to the woman. When your husband comes home each day, flops into a chair, sips his drink and silently watches television, you may accept this as the inevitable workingman's routine after a tiring day. But will you, too, at times find yourself resentful over this unwillingness to talk, especially when you have been confined to home and preschool children for seemingly weeks at a time?

To accept and adjust in these circumstances will take some giving.

Such an accepting-adjusting process (with its integral partner-compromise) begins in earnest on the wedding day and will last as long as the marriage does. A few specific areas in which this process should be operative deserve mention.

Finances. Money talks and is power. The person who signs checks controls a business. These observations may not necessarily apply to the home, but they do accentuate the importance of developing an efficient, mutually acceptable system of handling the family finances.

In-laws. After the matrimonial vows each person's prime commitment is to the marriage partner. But the responsibility to love, visit and care for parents continues. No exact rules or formulas exist for a harmonious settlement of this delicate question. Common sense, however, would urge that it be talked through with candor and thoroughness, particularly when serious illness incapacitates one of the parents.

Getting away together. A certain married man makes it a practice to get away at least once a month overnight with his wife and without the children. He feels the large sum for sitter, motel room, dinner and show represents a sound investment in a happy marriage. Routine deadens the freshness of all our relationships and such a break enables husband and wife to review and renew their own mutual love.

God is love and he has, in some mysterious way, drawn you together in love. But he leaves you free to make that love grow or allow it to slip backwards, to keep it alive or let it wither and die. The Lord will help you forge a fantastic future, if you do your share. A joy in marriage much beyond your expectations and a happiness exceeding by far that which you now experience lie ahead. The only requirement is your willingness to love, to give, to accept and to adjust. That condition, however, is a big one.

F-6 **Two Become One Body** (778-6)

Mark 10:6-9

**From the beginning of creation God
made them male and female.**

**This is why a man must leave father and
mother,**

**and the two become one body. They are
no longer two, therefore, but one body.**

**So then, what God has united, man must
not divide.**

This is the gospel of the Lord.

No Longer Two But One

Love, particularly married love, involves self-giving. In many ways on many occasions, it means putting aside one's own wishes and striving to fulfill the desires of another. When husband and wife engage in sexual intercourse it can, or should be, a most intimate instance of this, a time in which both totally forget self and concentrate on bringing pleasure to the other. Paradoxically, the success of their lovemaking will depend in large measure upon just how much each act is filled with a mutually unselfish concern for the other partner.

The husband plays a giving role here. He embraces, touches, caresses his wife; he carefully by words and actions prepares her for their physical union, creates within her a longing for him, stirs up a yearning in her that the two of them might become one body. Later, when they are in fact united as two in one flesh, he still gives. In a sense he only loans his body for intercourse, but the ejaculation of his seed within her is a total gift, a cannot-be-retracted donation of self. Afterwards, the considerate male companion continues this giving, carrying on his efforts with tender gesture and gentle whisper until his wife knows the same peace and satisfaction he now experiences.

The wife also does or should play an equally giving role. She may initiate the process leading to sexual intercourse or, if not, at least her reaction to his preliminary efforts certainly means a donation of self. So, too, the anxious opening of her heart and body and the active acceptance of him and of his gift within her require giving. In truth, unless she responds with warmth to his overtures and positively takes part in the entire action, her husband will sense disappointment, even frustration.

We might say, with greater accuracy, that marital love is not simply a giving, but a giving-receiving relationship. Successful sexual relations surely should be. The description above perhaps indicates in some general outline fashion how husband and wife both give during intercourse. But this represents only a theoretical sketch. For making love together is an extremely dynamic, personal affair. The give-take, giving-responding, donating-returning interplay varies so much that only the actual couple could describe who gives and how and in what way during their lovemaking.

Nor is it very important to analyze the process. What really counts is a wish in each partner's heart to please the other, to bring pleasure to the one loved. When that utter unconcern for self pervades sexual intercourse, then true joy abounds. In such an ideal, ecstatic relationship, complete oneness results. Husband and wife are carried out of themselves, sharing sensations and exchanging feelings, now giving, now receiving, now accepting, now responding.

That, however, is a model picture of sexual bliss in marriage. But it doesn't just happen.

F-7 **Marriage Feast of Cana** (778-7)

John 2:1-11

There was a wedding at Cana in Galilee.
The mother of Jesus was there,

and Jesus and his disciples had also
been invited.

When they ran out of wine, since the
wine provided for the wedding was all
finished, the mother of Jesus said to him,
"They have no wine."

Jesus said, "Woman, why turn to me? My
hour has not come yet."

His mother said to the servants, "Do
whatever he tells you."

There were six stone water jars standing
there, meant for the ablutions that are
customary among the Jews: each could
hold twenty or thirty gallons.

Jesus said to the servants, "Fill the jars
with water," and they filled them to
the brim.

"Draw some out now," he told them,
"and take it to the steward."

They did this; the steward tasted the
water, and it had turned into wine.
Having no idea where it came from—only
the servants who had drawn the water
knew—the steward called the bridegroom

and said, "People generally serve the
best wine first, and keep the cheaper sort
till the guests have had plenty to drink;
but you have kept the best wine till now."

This was the first of the signs given by
Jesus: it was given at Cana in Galilee.

He let his glory be seen and his disciples
believed in him.

This is the gospel of the Lord.

Mixed Marriages

In the musical *Fiddler on the Roof* the lovable Jewish father, already troubled by his children's and the community's departure from tradition, explodes when he learns his daughter wishes to marry a nonbeliever. Later, after hearing of their marriage, he rejects the girl, tells all she is gone, dead, forgotten, and warns that her name shall never again be mentioned in his home.

People in pluralistic America today take a somewhat more tolerant attitude toward mixed marriages. But the bitterness and heartbreak portrayed in the incident from *Fiddler* frequently find their way into the lives of those who love deeply, but believe differently. It is no one's fault. Certainly not the couple caught in the thorny situation and surely not the parents who have merely tried with great sincerity to transmit a cherished religious faith to their children.

Yet it does happen. Then a man and woman in love either must resolve their differences by some form of compromise or face the dreaded consequences of breaking up and following separate paths. Mere thought of the latter tears lovers apart; but the former also leaves something to be desired for no one walks away from a compromise fully satisfied.

If yours will be a mixed marriage, you presumably have already passed through that agonizing period and arrived at a livable solution. Have no fear. No life and no marriage are perfect. There are always differences to be accepted. Religious ones generally touch us more deeply and require a greater willingness to understand. But we can adjust to them, too, and even grow greatly in the process.

The real issue, however, centers not on the husband and wife but around the children who will come from this union. Two adults in love very likely could come to accept and respect each other's religious sentiments. Deciding on which faith to raise sons and daughters in is not settled so easily. That decision, nevertheless, should be reached whenever possible *before* a couple marries. To postpone this admittedly hard judgment until after the wedding will almost certainly create severe crises a few years later in marriage.

It helps to concentrate on those aspects of each other's beliefs which are shared in common and to learn as much as possible about the other's faith. A Catholic partner would do well to take the first step. Meeting the minister and congregation, occasionally attending a service, reading a little background material will facilitate future understanding and soothe present anxieties.

Recent changes in Church rules give to a couple in a mixed marriage the option of celebrating their wedding with a Nuptial Mass. Such a possibility may prove especially comforting to the Catholic woman who always has dreamed of this for her own marriage. But one can question if that represents the wisest alternative for all concerned. Given general restrictions on intercommunion, the fact a non-Catholic partner does not share Communion could serve to stress the split in religion rather than highlight the harmony of their love.

A much more satisfactory plan involves a scriptural marriage ceremony without Mass. The assisting minister, if there is one, may participate in this service by reading some of the biblical texts, offering prayers, giving an exhortation and bestowing a benediction. There are obvious advantages with such a rite and it eliminates the problem mentioned above. In addition, the Catholic party naturally can participate in the Eucharist at an earlier time during the day.

Differences need to be faced and accepted. Yet if a man and a woman love enough, they can adjust to those differences and enjoy an extremely happy life together in a mixed marriage.

F-8 Remain in My Love
(778-8)

John 15:9-12

Jesus said to his disciples:

"As the Father has loved me,
so I have loved you.
Remain in my love.

If you keep my commandments
you will remain in my love,
just as I have kept my Father's
    commandments
and remain in his love.

I have told you this
so that my own joy may be in you
and your joy be complete.

This is my commandment:
love one another
as I have loved you."

This is the gospel of the Lord.

F-9 Love One Another as I Have Loved You
(778-9)

John 15:12-16

Jesus said to his disciples:

"This is my commandment: Love one
another as I have loved you.

A man can have no greater love
than to lay down his life for his friends.

You are my friends,
if you do what I command you.

I shall not call you servants any more,
because a servant does not know
his master's business;
I call you friends,
because I have made known to you
everything I have learnt from my Father.

You did not choose me,
no, I chose you;
and I commissioned you
to go out and to bear fruit,
fruit that will last;
and then the Father will give you
anything you ask him in my name."

This is the gospel of the Lord.

Responsible Parenthood

To conceive and bring forth a child into the world is indeed a miracle. But the question plaguing many married couples today is how often that miracle should be repeated.

To make love and cooperate with God in the creation of new life also means to assume responsibility for this child through all his formative years. That is a heavy charge. Sometimes the tasks involved multiply and become so burdensome that a couple feels it would actually be wrong for them to have another child, as much as they would like to do so.

When Catholic bishops in Rome at the Second Vatican Council talked about human, Christian, responsible parenthood they were speaking of married people like this. *The Constitution on the Church in the Modern World* says, in effect, every couple should bear as many children as they can bring up into the world *and* properly bring up, and *only* that many. How many this will actually be remains a terribly personal decision reserved to husband and wife alone. The Fathers recognized that fact when they wrote: "The parents themselves should ultimately make this judgment in the sight of God. But in their manner of acting spouses should be aware that they cannot proceed arbitrarily."

Married persons seeking to decide in a proper way might ask themselves:

Are we being selfish? Is our decision to put off a child or an additional one prompted merely by a desire to have more time, money, freedom for ourselves?

Are we too trusting in God's providence? Have we blindly made love and expected that the Lord will provide in case a baby comes? God will, of course, supply what is wanting, but expects us to think and decide and act by ourselves as much as possible.

Are we not trusting enough in God's care? Every pregnancy and birth is a risk. Who knows what lies ahead in the future for mother or father or child? Sickness, death, unemployment? We cannot fully predict these things. While using all our human ingenuity to plan a family, on occasions we must simply leave the rest in the hands of God.

A futher difficulty at times develops for some married persons who have decided with prayer and thought, and without selfishness, that they should postpone temporarily or indefinitely the addition of a child to their family. They feel simultaneously a strong need to express and deepen love through sexual intercourse. Aware of the Church's traditional teaching and Pope Paul VI's encyclical they feel caught in a dilemma with God seeming to say one thing in their hearts and another through his Church. In resolving that issue they would do well to consider what new natural family planning techniques can offer. Information about these procedures, approved by the Church, tested with success, and free of harmful side effects, and the address of a local contact can be obtained from the Couple to Couple League National Office, P.O. Box 11084, Cincinnati, Ohio 45211.

There is no easy resolution of that matter, but neither does God want couples to be terrified whenever they make love. In the complexities of life all of us now and then become similarly torn between conflicting commands. At those times we purify our hearts, search for God's light in this special circumstance, then decide what is the best course to follow. And follow it without any fear or anxiety. Should you ever face such a situation and seem unable to cope with the conflict, then seek an understanding priest in or out of confession. He will not or should not make what must be your decision alone, but he can help you arrive at a judgment which will insure your continued peace with God and love for one another.

F-10 **That They May Be One as We Are One** (778-10)

Short version: John 17:20-23
Long version: John 17:20-26

verses 20-23

**Jesus raised his eyes to heaven and
prayed, saying:**

**"I pray not only for these,
but also for those
who through their words will believe in me.**

**May they all be one.
Father, may they be one in us,
as you are in me and I am in you,
so that the world may believe it was you
who sent me.**

**I have given them the glory you gave to me
that they may be one as we are one.**

**With me in them and you in me,
may they be so completely one
that the world will realize that it was you
who sent me
and that I have loved them as much as
you loved me.**

verses 24-26

**Father,
I want those you have given me
to be with me where I am,
so that they may always see the glory
you have given me
because you loved me
before the foundations of the world.**

**Father, Righteous One,
the world has not known you,
but I have known you,
and these have known
that you have sent me.**

**I have made your name known to them
and will continue to make it known,
so that the love with which you loved me
may be in them,
and so that I may be in them."**

This is the gospel of the Lord.

Completely One

Well-prepared books and pamphlets certainly can help newlyweds in their initial efforts at being one. At the same time, couples need not become preoccupied with mastering the "right" steps necessary for "perfect" sexual relations.

If the husband and wife possess one desire—to please the other—they cannot but succeed. And if on the wedding night the man is tender, gentle, yet confident and if the wife is trusting, relaxed, yet responsive, no serious difficulties should develop.

However, both of you must be patient. To make love is an art; to perfect it takes time. Together, with patience, you can grow, can learn and then soon you will not only make love, but will make love well.

Occasionally (not frequently) obstacles to a union of joy do arise. Normally these are settled very quickly with competent professional assistance. Should this happen in your case, don't suffer needlessly. A frightened young woman came for advice after six months of futile attempts to complete the sexual act with her husband. She was tortured by anxiety and crushed with disappointment. Swift and simple medical treatment easily eliminated the problem. Today they are proud parents and happy lovers, regretful only that they postponed seeking aid for so long.

Communication between husband and wife is essential for successful sex. The two of you should keep the channels of discussion clear and free, openly, honestly, sympathetically deciding what position is best, when seems the most suitable time, which methods bring the greatest pleasure.

Few rules restrict you here. Any action preceding intercourse you find mutually acceptable and not offensive to the sensibilities of the other is good, beautiful, pleasing to God.

For you the husband, self-giving love enters very strongly into this aspect of married life. You will achieve release and satisfaction in sexual intercourse without trouble, almost automatically. But for your wife, orgasm and total contentment come about in a much more complex fashion. Lovemaking for her is bound up with affection, getting attention, feeling needed, being properly stimulated. Your wife's cycle of excitation starts slower and lasts longer. She obtains an orgasm quite differently and perhaps less consistently than you do. It is not absolutely essential for her that she reach an orgasm on each occasion—merely bringing you peace and catering to your physical, emotional needs may satisfy her heart. But every effort should be made to enable her to experience full satisfaction.

The type of careful preparation demanded before actual intercourse will undoubtedly seem easy in the beginning. These caresses and embraces are new, exciting, unexplored territory. But everything in life dulls after repeated use and lovemaking is no exception. This will be your test as a good lover, as a considerate husband.

If, after the novelty wears off, you rush, perform routinely, then sexual intercourse will soon become a burden, not a blessing for your wife. She will feel you are taking her for granted, merely using her as a means of relieving your passions. She will come to dread sex as a duty. The marvel of it all will vanish. But if you are careful, if you lovingly prepare her for your entry, if you fight off the impulse to sleep and continue your lovemaking until she feels peace, then there will be no complaints. Then the two of you will be completely one in joy, in love, in happiness, happy together for life.

Rite of Marriage

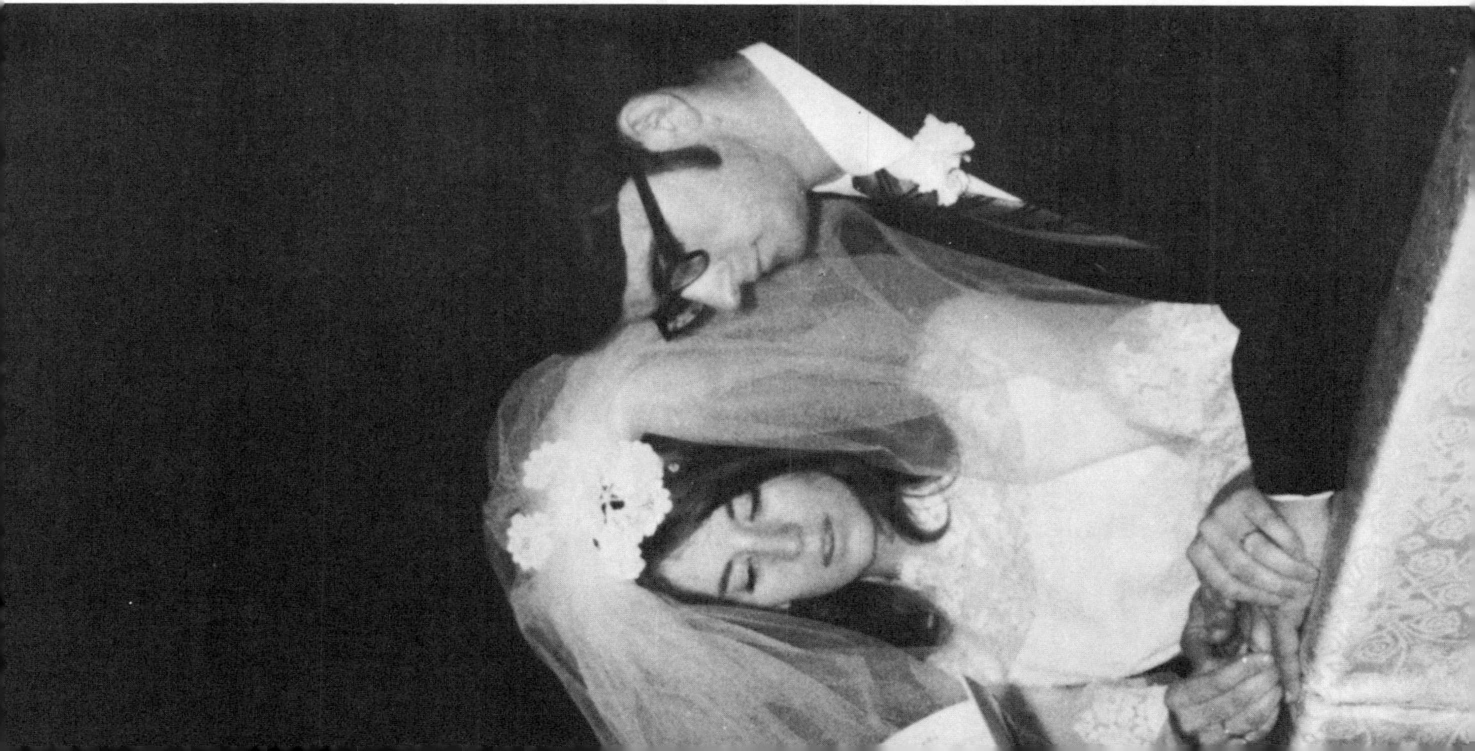

Introductory Address

23. *All stand, including the bride and bridegroom, and the priest addresses them in these or similar words:*

G-1

My dear friends,* you have come together in this church so that the Lord may seal and strengthen your love in the presence of the Church's minister and this community. Christ abundantly blesses this love. He has already consecrated you in baptism and now he enriches and strengthens you by a special sacrament so that you may assume the duties of marriage in mutual and lasting fidelity. And so, in the presence of the Church, I ask you to state your intentions.

Statement of Intentions

24. *The priest then questions them about their freedom of choice, faithfulness to each other, and the acceptance and upbringing of children:*

N. and N., have you come here freely and without reservation to give yourselves to each other in marriage?

Will you love and honor each other as man and wife for the rest of your lives?

The following questions may be omitted if, for example, the couple is advanced in years.

Will you accept children lovingly from God, and bring them up according to the law of Christ and his Church?

Each answers the questions separately.

Consent

25. *The priest invites the couple to declare their consent:*

H-1

Since it is your intention to enter into marriage, join your right hands, and declare your consent before God and his Church.

They join hands.
The bridegroom says:

I, N., take you, N., to be my wife. I promise to be true to you in good times and in bad, in sickness and in health. I will love you and honor you all the days of my life.

---

*At the discretion of the priest, other words which seem more suitable under the circumstances, such as friends, dearly beloved, brethren, may be used. This also applies to parallel instances in the liturgy.

The bride says:

I, N., take you, N., to be my husband. I promise to be true to you in good times and in bad, in sickness and in health. I will love you and honor you all the days of my life.

If, however, it seems preferable for pastoral reasons, the priest may obtain consent from the couple through questions.

First he asks the bridegroom:

N., do you take N. to be your wife? Do you promise to be true to her in good times and in bad, in sickness and in health, to love her and honor her all the days of your life?

The bridegroom: **I do.**

Then he asks the bride:

N., do you take N. to be your husband? Do you promise to be true to him in good times and in bad, in sickness and in health, to love him and honor him all the days of your life?

The bride: **I do.**

H-2

In the dioceses of the United States, the following alternative form may be used:

I, N., take you, N., for my lawful wife (husband), to have and to hold, from this day forward, for better, for worse, for richer, for poorer, in sickness and in health, until death do us part.

If it seems preferable for pastoral reasons for the priest to obtain consent from the couple through questions, in the dioceses of the United States the following alternative form may be used:

N., do you take N. for your lawful wife (husband), to have and to hold, from this day forward, for better, for worse, for richer, for poorer, in sickness and in health, until death do you part?

R. **I do.**

Reception of Consent

26. *Receiving their consent, the priest says:*

You have declared your consent before the Church. May the Lord in his goodness strengthen your consent and fill you both with his blessings.

What God has joined, men must not divide.

R. Amen.

Blessing and Exchange of Rings

I-1

27. Priest:

May the Lord bless + these rings
which you give to each other
as the sign of your love and fidelity.

27a(47a)

R. Amen.

Other forms of the blessing of rings:

I-2

Lord, bless these rings which we bless + in your name.
Grant that those who wear them
may always have a deep faith in each other.
May they do your will
and always live together
in peace, good will, and love.

27b(110)

(We ask this) through Christ our Lord.

R. Amen.

I-3

Lord,
bless + and consecrate N. and N.
in their love for each other.
May these rings be a symbol
of true faith in each other,
and always remind them of their love.

27c(111)

Through Christ our Lord.

R. Amen.

28. The bridegroom places his wife's ring on her ring finger. He may say:

N., take this ring as a sign of my love and fidelity. In the name of the
Father, and of the Son, and of the Holy Spirit.

The bride places her husband's ring on his ring finger. She may say:

N., take this ring as a sign of my love and fidelity. In the name of the
Father, and of the Son, and of the Holy Spirit.

Prayer of the Couple (optional)

After the exchange of vows and ring(s), during thanksgiving after communion, or at another appropriate time you may, if you wish, recite together a brief and personally composed prayer to God the Father. It basically will be the expression of your wish for the Lord's blessing and protection on this marriage. You can prepare this in advance on a small card and have the priest hand it to you at the proper moment.

Something entirely personal is best. However, if you would like to use the prayer of the couple yet feel awkward about writing your own, the following example may be helpful:

O God, our Father in heaven, we now kneel before you very happy, but somewhat nervous. We feel you brought us together in the beginning, helped our love grow and at this moment are with us in a special way. We ask that you stay by our side in the days ahead. Protect us from anything which might harm this marriage, give us courage when burdens come our way, teach us to forgive one another when we fail.

(For the groom:)
I ask from you the assistance I need to be a good husband and father. Never let me take my wife for granted or forget she needs to be loved. If you bless us with children, I promise to love them, to care for them, to give them the best possible example.

(For the bride:)
I ask from you the assistance I need to be a good wife and mother. May I never fail to give my husband encouragement. If you bless me with motherhood, I promise to give myself totally to the children, even to the point of stepping aside when they must walk alone.

We ask, finally, that in our old age we may love one another as deeply and cherish each other as much as we do at this very moment. May you grant these wishes which we offer through your Son, Jesus Christ, our Lord and Savior.

Prayer of the Faithful

29. The general intercessions (prayer of the faithful) follow, using formulas approved by the conference of bishops. If the rubrics call for it, the profession of faith is said after the general intercessions.

The marriage ceremony centers around you as bride and groom. But even at this time you cannot become self-centered and forget the needs of others in the world. As with the prayer of the couple, you many compose your own prayer of the faithful (this is the ideal) or use one of the three provided here.

J-1

Priest: (In these or similar words)
Now that we have heard God's word in the Bible and felt his Presence in this exchange of vows, let us present to God the Father these petitions for people in the world today.

(The following intentions could be recited by the couple, a parent, relative or friend. The response of the congregation will vary from place to place and should be indicated to the people present.)

1. For our Holy Father on earth, the Pope, all the bishops and the clergy everywhere that they may lead us to deeper faith in God and a stronger love for others, let us pray to the Lord.

2. For our president and all leaders of government that they may be effective in achieving peace and eliminating poverty, let us pray to the Lord.

3. For married persons that they may continue to give, be able to forgive and find happiness deepen with the passing of each day, let us pray to the Lord.

4. For N. and N., now beginning their life together, that they may have divine assistance at every moment, the constant support of friends, the rich blessing of children, a warm love reaching out to others and good health until a ripe old age, let us pray to the Lord.

5. For those who are sick, lonely, discouraged or oppressed that they may be strengthened by God's help and aided by their friends, let us pray to the Lord.

6. For those who have died, especially the relatives and friends of N. and N. and of all present for this wedding, that they may enjoy perfect happiness and total fulfillment in eternal life, let us pray to the Lord.

7. For these personal needs which we mention now in silence (pause), let us pray to the Lord.

Priest: (The celebrant may use this or compose a suitable summary prayer with the conclusion . . . through Christ our Lord.)

O God our Father in heaven, your Son taught us to ask, to seek and to knock. We have just done so, confident that you will now look upon our many needs, consider our trusting faith, and in your great love grant these requests which we present to you through Jesus Christ our Lord.

All. Amen.

Priest:

**We have listened to the word of God.
Let us now ask God to listen to us,
to bless our words of prayer
which we offer
for the people of the world.**

Reader: **The response is "Lord, hear our
prayer."**

**For leaders of Church and State
for heads of institutions
for heads of homes and households . . .
that they will lead us and guide us
in the search for God and the good life
in the search for peace and joy
in the search for love among us—
let us pray to the Lord.**

**For all married people:
for those who married yesterday
for the new couple, N. and N., married
today
for those who will marry tomorrow . . .
that they may savor
the joy of being together
warm love and children
a long life, wine, and friends
and a new day, every day—
let us pray to the Lord.**

**For all young single people
who look forward to a vocation
full of life and full of love—
let us pray to the Lord.**

**For the lonely old and the lonely young
for the hungry rich man
and the hungry poor man
for the sick in body, mind, and spirit
for the weak man in all of us—
let us pray to the Lord.**

**For our relatives and friends
who walk with us on life's journey
and for those who have gone before us
to the other side of life.
For the fulfillment of all their unfulfilled
desires—
let us pray to the Lord.**

Priest:

**These are our words of prayer today
for ourselves and all human beings.
Tomorrow there will be others.
Lord God the beloved of humankind
who has first loved us
give our words by your listening
the power of your word
so that all things may be accomplished
sweetly and gently
for the happiness of all.
Through Christ our Lord.** (ESG)

People: Amen.

God has given us His promises in the word of Scripture. N. (bride) and N. (groom) have given their promises to each other in their marriage. This hour of promise is also a time of prayer. We turn to God our Father and make our response by saying (singing): "Lord, have mercy."

> For our Church, to keep the promise of salvation, we pray to the Lord.
>
> For our world, to keep the promise of peace, we pray to the Lord.
>
> For our country, to keep the promise of freedom, we pray to the Lord.
>
> For our parish, to keep the promise of discipleship, we pray to the Lord.
>
> For our hearts, to keep the promise of loving, we pray to the Lord.
>
> For our hands, to keep the promise of giving, we pray to the Lord.
>
> For our lives, to keep the promise of growing, we pray to the Lord.
>
> For this couple, to keep the promise of marriage, we pray to the Lord.

Concluding Prayer

Father, You have chosen us and given us Your love, the power of the Holy Spirit in our midst. Hear our prayers today and keep us open. May our faith issue forth in action, our love show itself in deeds, and our hope give us courage. We ask this through Christ our Lord. Amen.

(WF)

The Liturgy of the Eucharist

Prayer Over the Gifts

K-1

Lord,
accept our offering
for this newly married couple, N. and N.
By your love and providence you have brought them together;
now bless them all the days of their married life.

(We ask this) through Christ our Lord.

112

K-2

Lord,
accept the gifts we offer you
on this happy day.
In your fatherly love
watch over and protect N. and N.,
whom you have united in marriage.

(We ask this) through Christ our Lord.

113

K-3

Lord,
hear our prayers
and accept the gifts we offer for N. and N.
Today you have made them one in the sacrament of marriage.
May the mystery of Christ's unselfish love,
which we celebrate in this eucharist,
increase their love for you and for each other.

(We ask this) through Christ our Lord.

114

Preface

L-1

Father, all-powerful and ever-living God, 115
we do well always and everywhere to give you thanks.
By this sacrament your grace unites man and woman
in an unbreakable bond of love and peace.

You have designed the chaste love of husband and wife
for the increase both of the human family
and of your own family born in baptism.

You are the loving Father of the world of nature;
you are the loving Father of the new creation of grace.
In Christian marriage you bring together the two orders of creation:
nature's gift of children enriches the world
and your grace enriches also your Church.

Through Christ the choirs of angels
and all the saints
praise and worship your glory.
May our voices blend with theirs
as we join in their unending hymn:

L-2

Father, all-powerful and ever-living God, 116
we do well always and everywhere to give you thanks
through Jesus Christ our Lord.

Through him you entered into a new covenant with your people.
You restored man to grace in the saving mystery of redemption.
You gave him a share in the divine life
through his union with Christ.
You made him an heir of Christ's eternal glory.

This outpouring of love in the new covenant of grace
is symbolized in the marriage covenant
that seals the love of husband and wife
and reflects your divine plan of love.

And so, with the angels and all the saints in heaven
we proclaim your glory
and join in their unending hymn of praise:

Father, all-powerful and ever-living God,   117
we do well always and everywhere to give you thanks.

You created man in love to share your divine life.
We see his high destiny in the love of husband and wife,
which bears the imprint of your own divine love.

Love is man's origin,
love is his constant calling,
love is his fulfillment in heaven.

The love of man and woman
is made holy in the sacrament of marriage,
and becomes the mirror of your everlasting love.

Through Christ the choirs of angels
and all the saints
praise and worship your glory.
May our voices blend with theirs
as we join in their unending hymn:

Nuptial Blessing

33. *After the Lord's Prayer, the prayer* Deliver us *is omitted.* *The priest faces the bride and bridegroom and, with hands joined, says:*

M-1

My dear friends, let us turn to the Lord and pray   119 (33a)
that he will bless with his grace this woman (or N.)
now married in Christ to this man (or N.)
and that (through the sacrament of the body and blood of Christ)
he will unite in love the couple he has joined in this holy bond.

All pray silently for a short while. *Then the priest extends his hands and continues:*

Father, by your power you have made everything out of nothing.
In the beginning you created the universe
and made mankind in your own likeness.
You gave man the constant help of woman
so that man and woman should no longer be two, but one flesh,
and you teach us that what you have united
may never be divided.

Father, you have made the union of man and wife so holy a mystery
that it symbolizes the marriage of Christ and his Church.

Father, by your plan man and woman are united,
and married life has been established
as the one blessing that was not forfeited by original sin
or washed away in the flood.

Look with love upon this woman, your daughter,
now joined to her husband in marriage.
She asks your blessing.
Give her the grace of love and peace.

May she always follow the example of the holy women
whose praises are sung in the scriptures.

May her husband put his trust in her
and recognize that she is his equal
and the heir with him to the life of grace.
May he always honor her and love her
as Christ loves his bride, the Church.

Father, keep them always true to your commandments.
Keep them faithful in marriage
and let them be living examples of Christian life.

Give them the strength which comes from the gospel
so that they may be witnesses of Christ to others.
(Bless them with children
and help them to be good parents.
May they live to see their children's children.)

And, after a happy old age,
grant them fullness of life with the saints
in the kingdom of heaven.

(We ask this) through Christ our Lord.

R. Amen.

34. *If one or both of the parties will not be receiving communion, the words in the introduction to the nuptial blessing,* through the sacrament of the body and blood of Christ, *may be omitted.*

If desired, in the prayer Father, by your power, *two of the first three paragraphs may be omitted, keeping only the paragraph which corresponds to the reading of the Mass.*

In the last paragraph of this prayer, the words in parentheses may be omitted whenever circumstances suggest it, if, for example, the couple is advanced in years.

Other forms of the nuptial blessing:

In the following prayer, either the paragraph Holy Father, you created mankind *or the paragraph* Father, to reveal the plan of your love, *may be omitted, keeping only the paragraph which corresponds to the reading of the Mass.*

M-2

Let us pray to the Lord for N. and N. 120 (34b)
who come to God's altar at the beginning of their married life
so that they may always be united in love for each other
(as now they share in the body and blood of Christ).

All pray silently for a short while. Then the priest extends his hands and continues:

Holy Father, you created mankind in your own image
and made man and woman to be joined as husband and wife
in union of body and heart
and so fulfill their mission in this world.

Father, to reveal the plan of your love,
you made the union of husband and wife
an image of the covenant between you and your people.

In the fulfillment of this sacrament,
the marriage of Christian man and woman
is a sign of the marriage between Christ and the Church.
Father, stretch out your hand, and bless N. and N.

Lord, grant that as they begin to live this sacrament
they may share with each other the gifts of your love
and become one in heart and mind
as witnesses to your presence in their marriage.
Help them to create a home together
(and give them children to be formed by the gospel
and to have a place in your family).

Give your blessings to N., your daughter,
so that she may be a good wife (and mother),
caring for the home,
faithful in love for her husband,
generous and kind.
Give your blessings to N., your son,
so that he may be a faithful husband
(and a good father).

Father, grant that as they come together to your table on earth,
so they may one day have the joy of sharing your feast in heaven.

(We ask this) through Christ our Lord.

R. Amen.

M-3

My dear friends, let us ask God   121 (34c)
for his continued blessings upon this bridegroom and his bride
(or N. and N.).

*All pray silently for a short while. Then the priest extends his hands and
continues:*

Holy Father, creator of the universe,
maker of man and woman in your own likeness,
source of blessing for married life,
we humbly pray to you for this woman
who today is united with her husband in this sacrament of marriage.

May your fullest blessing come upon her and her husband
so that they may together rejoice in your gift of married love
(and enrich your Church with their children).

Lord, may they both praise you when they are happy
and turn to you in their sorrows.
May they be glad that you help them in their work
and know that you are with them in their need.
May they pray to you in the community of the Church,
and be your witnesses in the world.
May they reach old age in the company of their friends,
and come at last to the kingdom of heaven.

(We ask this) through Christ our Lord.

R. Amen.

35. *At the words* Let us offer each other the sign of peace, *the married couple
and all present show their peace and love for one another in an
appropriate way.*

Prayer After Communion

N-1

Lord,
in your love
you have given us this eucharist
to unite us with one another and with you.
As you have made N. and N.
one in this sacrament of marriage
(and in the sharing of the one bread and the one cup),
so now make them one in love for each other.

(We ask this) through Christ our Lord.

122

N-2

Lord,
we who have shared the food of your table
pray for our friends N. and N.,
whom you have joined together in marriage.
Keep them close to you always.
May their love for each other
proclaim to all the world
their faith in you.

(We ask this) through Christ our Lord.

123

N-3

Almighty God,
may the sacrifice we have offered
and the eucharist we have shared
strengthen the love of N. and N.,
and give us all your fatherly aid.

(We ask this) through Christ our Lord.

124

Concluding Rite
Final Blessing

37. *Before blessing the people at the end of Mass, the priest blesses the*
bride and bridegroom, using one of the forms below:

O-1

God the eternal Father keep you in love with each other,   125 (37a)
so that the peace of Christ may stay with you
and be always in your home.

R. *Amen.*

May (your children bless you,)
your friends console you
and all men live in peace with you.

R. *Amen.*

May you always bear witness to the love of God in this world
so that the afflicted and the needy
will find in you generous friends,
and welcome you into the joys of heaven.

R. *Amen.*

And may almighty God bless you all,
the Father, and the Son, + and the Holy Spirit.

R. *Amen.*

O-2

May God, the almighty Father,   126 (37b)
give you his joy
and bless you (in your children).

R. *Amen.*

May the only Son of God have mercy on you
and help you in good times and in bad.

R. *Amen.*

May the Holy Spirit of God
always fill your hearts with his love.

R. *Amen.*

And may almighty God bless you all,
the Father, and the Son, + and the Holy Spirit.

R. *Amen.*

O-3

May the Lord Jesus, who was a guest at the wedding in Cana,   127 (37c)
bless you and your families and friends.

R.   Amen.

May Jesus, who loved his Church to the end,
always fill your hearts with his love.

R.   Amen.

May he grant that, as you believe in his resurrection,
so you may wait for him in joy and hope.

R.   Amen.

And may almighty God bless you all,
the Father, and the Son, $+$ and the Holy Spirit.

R.   Amen.

O-4

Alternate Final Blessing (in the United States)

May almighty God, with his words of blessing, unite your hearts in the
never-ending bond of pure love.

R.   Amen.

May your children bring you happiness, and may your generous
love for them be returned to you, many times over.

R.   Amen.

May the peace of Christ live always in your hearts and in your home.
May you have true friends to stand by you, both in joy and in sorrow.
May you be ready and willing to help and comfort all who come to you
in need.
And may the blessings promised to the compassionate be yours in
abundance.

May you find happiness and satisfaction in your work.
May daily problems never cause you undue anxiety, nor the desire for
earthly possessions dominate your lives.
But may your hearts' first desire be always the good things waiting for
you in the life of heaven.

R.   Amen.

May the Lord bless you with many happy years together, so that you
may enjoy the rewards of a good life.
And after you have served him loyally in his kingdom on earth,
may he welcome you to his eternal kingdom in heaven.

R.   Amen.

Importance and Dignity of the Sacrament of Matrimony

1. Married Christians, in virtue of the sacrament of matrimony, signify and share in the mystery of that unity and fruitful love which exists between Christ and his Church; they help each other to attain to holiness in their married life and in the rearing and education of their children; and they have their own special gift among the people of God.

2. Marriage arises in the covenant of marriage, or irrevocable consent, which each partner freely bestows on and accepts from the other. This intimate union and the good of the children impose total fidelity on each of them and argue for an unbreakable oneness between them. Christ the Lord raised this union to the dignity of a sacrament so that it might more clearly recall and more easily reflect his own unbreakable union with his Church.

3. Christian couples, therefore, nourish and develop their marriage by undivided affection, which wells up from the fountain of divine love, while, in a merging of human and divine love, they remain faithful in body and in mind, in good times as in bad.

4. By their very nature, the institution of matrimony and wedded love are ordained for the procreation and education of children and find in them their ultimate crown. Therefore, married Christians, while not considering the other purposes of marriage of less account, should be steadfast and ready to cooperate with the love of the Creator and Savior, who through them will constantly enrich and enlarge his own family.

5. A priest should bear in mind these principles of faith, both in his instructions to those about to be married and when giving the homily during the marriage ceremony. He should relate his instructions to the texts of the sacred readings.

   The bridal couple should be given a review of the fundamentals of Christian doctrine. This may include instruction on the teachings about marriage and the family, on the rites used in the celebration of the sacrament itself, and on the prayers and readings. In this way the bridegroom and the bride will receive far greater benefit from the celebration.

6. In the celebration of marriage (which normally should be within the Mass), certain elements should be stressed, especially the liturgy of the word, which shows the importance of Christian marriage in the history of salvation and the duties and responsibility of the couple in caring for the holiness of their children. Also of supreme importance are the consent of the contracting parties, which the priest asks and receives; the special nuptial blessing for the bride and for the marriage covenant; and finally, the reception of holy communion by the groom and the bride, and by all present, by which their love is nourished and all are lifted up into communion with our Lord and with one another.

7. Priests should first of all strengthen and nourish the faith of those about to be married, for the sacrament of matrimony presupposes and demands faith.

Interfaith Marriages

My Episcopalian father died of cancer when I was six. A few years later my mother met and eventually married a fine Christian gentleman, but her new husband, like the previous one, was not a Roman Catholic. They exchanged nuptial vows before a priest, but quietly in the rectory according to the standard procedure of the Catholic Church in the United States during those early 1940's.

A decade after this ceremony my brother took unto himself a lovely bride, a girl who, for the most part, grew up in the South and was raised by her parents in the Protestant tradition. Chuck and his fiancee made their life-lasting promises in the presence of a Catholic clergyman, but they did so inside St. Gabriel's Church, although outside the sanctuary area. The rules for mixed marriages, you see, had changed in those ten years.

By the time I was ordained a priest in 1956 the regulations had been altered a bit further. Now all couples, with few exceptions, entered within the sanctuary, stood before the altar, and vowed to live together in love "until death do us part." Shortly thereafter, Church authorities permitted bride and groom in a mixed or interfaith union to celebrate their marriage at a Mass with the Catholic partner receiving a special nuptial blessing previously reserved for occasions in which both spouses were Roman Catholic.

Why were the laws in the past so strict and seemingly unfair or discriminatory? What brought about these numerous changes in such a relatively brief period of time?

The answer to that first inquiry can be found, basically, in these words from the latest Roman Catholic document on this subject. "The Church greatly desires that Catholics marry Catholics and generally discourages mixed marriages." Tough, perhaps offensive, words, aren't they, particularly when two feel so close, so one in love, even though their religious beliefs and practices differ greatly?

But in honesty we must admit that such differences do cause tension and require added adjustment, greater giving on the part of both husband and wife. I should know. I am a product of a mixed marriage and spent my first 25 years in a home which was filled with love, deep in happiness, yet divided by religion.

Those tight rules of earlier days sought to impress upon starry-eyed lovers that love is beautiful, but sometimes blind, that love doesn't really conquer all, that it takes more effort to be fully one and perfectly united when you worship at separate churches Sunday after Sunday.

However, hard statistics tell us this: Men and women with different religious backgrounds continue on an ever-increasing scale to fall in love and wish to spend the rest of their lives together. The Catholic Church seeks to cope with these realities and lend those couples special help and support.

It also recognizes that rigid rules in a complex modern world just won't do. The gradual shift in approach I have described above and the further developments I will outline below reflect an awareness of our contemporary scene. These principles hold up the religious ideal of a Catholic marrying a Catholic (or a Protestant, a Protestant; a Jew, a Jew), but deal sensibly and, I think, in an understanding, warm way, with lovers who find themselves in a mixed or interfaith situation.

Pope Paul VI issued in 1970 an "Apostolic Letter Determining Norms for Mixed Marriages." In that decree he left many decisions to the hierarchy of each country; our own National Conference of Catholic Bishops applied the Pope's guidelines to the United States in a document which took effect January 1, 1971. Their statement covers the following important questions, items which you and your partner undoubtedly have been concerned about, if you contemplate or actually are preparing for an interfaith marriage.

Who will help us get ready spiritually for the marriage and, specifically, for the wedding ceremony?

The American norms state: "In the assistance which he gives in preparation for marriage between a Catholic and a non-Catholic, and his continued efforts to help all married couples and families, the priest should endeavor to be in contact and to cooperate with the minister or religious counselor of the non-Catholic."

The Catholic priest, then, ought to take the initiative by enlisting the assistance of ministers or religious counselors from other traditions in preparing couples for marriage. You will find two additional sections in this booklet (comment on Reading No. D-10, "Dressed in Dazzling White," and comment on Reading No. F-7, "Mixed Marriages") which offer practical suggestions along this line and also touch other areas of great concern.

What about our future children?

The Catholic Church views the faith of its members as a precious gift, a treasure to be handed down, where possible, to the children. The new regulations, consequently, require the Catholic ordinarily to make either in writing or orally a promise to that effect in these or similar words:

"I reaffirm my faith in Jesus Christ and, with God's help, intend to continue living that faith in the Catholic Church. I promise to do all in my power to share the faith I have received with our children by having them baptized and reared as Catholics."

The partner who is not Roman Catholic neither signs papers nor is asked to make promises about bringing the children up Catholic. However, he or she naturally should be informed of and understand his or her spouse's obligations in this regard. If a couple has particularly serious problems over the issue of their future children's religious training, they should consult with a parish priest. He will refer cases which cannot be resolved satisfactorily in the usual fashion to his bishop for a decision.

In this sometimes thorny matter, couples would do well to recall these words of the bishops' statement. "In reaching a concrete decision concerning the baptism and religious education of children, both partners should remember that neither thereby abdicates the fundamental responsibility of parents to see that their children are instilled with deep and abiding religious values. . . ."

Where may we have the wedding ceremony?

You may, of course, celebrate your vows in a Catholic church, either in the context of a nuptial Mass or outside Mass. The revised Roman Catholic ritual provides for either arrangement a rich variety of scriptural readings plus biblically oriented prayers and blessings from which to choose that could be ideally suited to your needs. The regular edition of *Together for Life* contains the entire rite for marriage, including all texts needed for a ceremony either within or outside Mass. *Together for Life—special edition for marriage outside Mass* has been edited, and will prove particularly helpful, for use in a nuptial service outside Mass. In any case, as we have mentioned elsewhere, joint participation by priest and minister in the Catholic ceremony can prove extremely effective as a sign of common sharing in the midst of differences.

If, however, a good reason exists (e.g., the Protestant bride wishes to be married in her own church, one partner has a minister who is a relative or close friend), the local bishop may permit the Catholic spouse to be married outside a Catholic church and before someone other than a priest. In such an arrangement, the priest might very well join in the ceremony with the other clergyman.

Does the wedding have to take place in church or be a religious service?

Always, no; generally, yes. When a bishop permits the nuptial ceremony to be celebrated outside a Catholic church, he usually and understandably envisions a religious marriage service and one which takes place in a church. However, once again, we enjoy today a true flexibility of approach. In exceptional circumstances, a civil ceremony may be necessary and is allowed for the good of all involved. Similarly, in other situations, it may not be best to insist on the religious service in a church. The bishop may also approve this possibility.

In a word, under current legislation the parish priest or local bishop now, fortunately, can resolve with ease and swiftness any conflict or controversy arising over the who and where of the wedding service.

May we write our own ceremony?

Again, yes and no. For couples marrying according to the Catholic ritual, we encourage them to plan together a nuptial liturgy and, within certain minor limits, to prepare creatively a wedding rite which will be distinctively their own. If bride and groom exchange vows before some clergyman other than a priest, they will presumably follow the minister's ritual with whatever freedom it offers to the couple in terms of choice and creativity.

Below you will find, as something of a sample, excerpts from the recently revised liturgies for marriage of the Episcopal and Presbyterian Churches in the United States.

God the Father, God the Son, God the Holy Spirit, bless, preserve and keep you; the Lord mercifully with his favor, look upon you and fill you with all spiritual benediction and grace, that you may faithfully live together in this life, and in the world to come have life everlasting. Amen.[1]

Eternal God: without your grace no promise is sure. Strengthen .... and .... with the gift of your Spirit, so they may fulfill the vows they have taken. Keep them faithful to each other and to you. Fill them with such love and joy that they may build a home where no one is a stranger. And guide them by your word to serve you all the days of their lives; through Jesus Christ our Lord, to whom be honor and glory forever and ever. Amen.[2]

---

[1] "The Celebration and Blessing of a Marriage" from *Pastoral Offices, Prayer Book Studies 24.* Forms and services prepared by the Standing Liturgical Commission of the Episcopal Church. Published by The Church Hymnal Corporation, 800 Second Avenue, New York, N.Y. 10017. Copyright © 1970 by Charles Mortimer Guilbert.
[2] "The Marriage Service" from *The Worshipbook Services.* Prepared by The Joint Committee on Worship for Cumberland Presbyterian Church, Presbyterian Church in the United States, the United Presbyterian Church in the United States of America. Copyright © MCMLXX by The Westminster Press. Used by permission.

RECORD OF SELECTIONS

*These were the readings, prayers, and blessings
which we selected for our marriage ceremony.*

Opening Prayer (A1-4) page 7   No. ....

Old Testament Reading (B1-8) pages 10-24   No. ....

Responsorial Psalm (C1-7) pages 26-29   No. ....

New Testament Reading (D1-10) pages 32-48   No. ....

Alleluia Verse and
    Verse Before the Gospel (E1-4) page 48   No. ....

Gospel Reading (F1-10) pages 52-68   No. ....

Exchange of Consent (H1-2) pages 72-73   No. ....

Blessing of the Rings (I1-5) page 74   No. ....

Prayer of the Couple: Yes .... No ....

       Formula on page 75   ....

       Personally composed formula   ....

Prayer of the Faithful:

       Formula (J1-3) on pages 76-78   ....

       Personally composed formula   ....

       Formula prepared by priest   ....

Prayer Over the Gifts (K1-3) page 80   No. ....

Preface (L1-3) pages 81-82   No. ....

Nuptial Blessing (M1-3) pages 83-85   No. ....

Prayer After Communion (N1-3) page 86   No. ....

Final Blessing (O1-4) pages 87-88   No. ....

MARRIAGE RECORD

We

_____ *and* _____

received from each other the Holy Sacrament of Matrimony

on _____*at*_____

The priest who witnessed our marriage was _____

The best man and the bridesmaid who witnessed our marriage were

_____ *and* _____

Other attendants

_____   _____

_____   _____

GROOM'S PARENTS   BRIDE'S PARENTS

_____   _____

_____   _____